bold ink

Collected Voices of Women and Girls

WriteGirl Publications
WriteGirl

4003 Sunset Drive, #9
Los Angeles, CA 90027
http://www.writegirl.org

bold ink: *Collected Voices of Women and Girls / WriteGirl*
ISBN 0-9741251-0-5

Editors **Deborah Reber & Keren Taylor**

Art Direction **Keren Taylor**

Book Design **Juliana Sankaran-Felix**

Cover Art **Girl Blue**, mixed media 11 1/2 x 9 in. by **Keren Taylor**

Cover Design **Sara Apelkvist & Keren Taylor**

Photographs courtesy of **Stephanie Bowen, Deborah Reber & Keren Taylor.**

Never Underestimate The power of a Girl and her pen.

acknowledgements

Nine months in the making, this book you are holding had a great team of people assisting along the way.

A huge thank you to our editorial crew, who worked wonders in record time: Allison Deegan, Christine McBride, Jennifer Repo and Diane Saltzberg. And a special thank you to Allison for her complete dedication, attention to detail and awesome big-picture perspective in the completion of this book.

Thank you to writers Chris Culler, Sheana Ochoa, Pat Payne and Jennifer Repo for their contributions to Chapter VI: This is WriteGirl.

Thanks to Dipali Murti and Amaela Wiley for their insight in the early phases of development for *Bold Ink*.

We are extremely grateful to our book designer, Juliana Sankaran-Felix, for her unwavering commitment to this project, her flexibility through all our changes and her creative aesthetics in creating a place for these voices to live.

Note from Keren to Debbie — you've been just fantastic to work with on this book. Thank you for your patience, your focus, your creative insights and your sense of humor.

Note from Debbie to Keren — thanks for trusting me with this project...it's been a wonderful journey together!

We thank the Bresee Community Center for hosting our monthly creative writing workshops — there couldn't be a more welcoming staff. And for all her enthusiastic support throughout this journey, we thank Lori Obregon, Director of Literacy & Enrichment, Bresee Foundation.

Thank you to our nonprofit incubator, Community Partners, and its warm staff for help with the seemingly endless details in developing this publishing arm of WriteGirl.

To Sara Apelkvist and Fabric Interactive, we extend a huge thanks for strategy and design in developing the face of WriteGirl in printed materials and on the web.

Many thanks to the terrific staff at the Writers Guild of America, west and the Writers Guild Foundation for assistance in promoting Bold Ink to the writing community.

To our enthusiastic Advisory Board, thank you for your guidance and support, which has been invaluable in making WriteGirl, and this anthology, a reality.

To honorary "WriteBoys" – our husbands, Derin Basden and Jacques Henri Taylor, thank you for your endless support.

And to all the WriteGirls who contributed their work to this anthology, thank you for sharing a piece of yourselves, challenging us to be the tenacious communicators we vowed to be and giving us a chance to make the WriteGirl magic work for you. You are bold, you are hilarious, you are intriguing, and you are published!

Deborah Reber & Keren Taylor

table of contents

I: THIS IS ME

II: THIS IS US

III: THE VIEW FROM HERE

III: THE VIEW FROM HERE *(continued)*

IV: THIS INSPIRES ME

9

V: GREAT ESCAPES

VI: THIS IS WRITEGIRL

foreword

From the moment Keren Taylor asked me to be on the board of WriteGirl in December 2001, I was hooked. Women writers mentoring teenage girls in central Los Angeles. What a fantastic idea! Yes, I told her, I want to be involved in this.

I realized that Keren's new organization could offer girls the most important thing they need in their teenage years: a voice. The mentors would inspire the girls, guide them to find their own voices and assure them that nothing was too wild or crazy or ordinary to put on the page. What I didn't realize was how successful Keren's dream would be — how deeply it would reach into the community, the talent it would unearth, and how quickly it would grow.

At my first introduction to WriteGirl in action, I could feel excitement and energy bouncing off the walls at the Bresee Community Center. Just tables and chairs filled the room, paper and pencils on the tables. But more than anything, I remember the overwhelming girl power, word power, story power. WriteGirl is having your secret thoughts, fantasies and experiences accepted, but it's also about stretching toward your own dreams through your imagination. What could be more empowering, more fun, for both mentors and mentees? The force that generated all this energy of course is Keren Taylor — who had her own dream and made it come true. What a role model for the girls!

The girls' voices fill the pages of this wonderful book, writing of their real lives as well as lives they imagine. These vibrant voices include Glenda Garcia writing about all the disillusions she was old enough for: *"I was old enough to see my mom struggle trying to get ahead and always ending in the same spot."* In "@9:56" Mariana Vásquez writes a poem illuminating one ordinary moment that ends with the lines: *"Some guyz on their skateboards,/Trying to do tricks./Two little girls laughing, /Laughing at their feet./My mom watches a movie/and me, I'm just writing this/@9:56."* In her poem "Sunday Dress," Perla Melendez takes us into the mind and heart of a homeless woman photographed by Dorothea Lange during the Depression: *"Wearing her best clothes/Which were her only clothes, really/Which were her Sunday clothes/ Or, what used to be her Sunday clothes/Back when there were still Sundays."* Alma Castrejon writes a poem full of anger and admiration to Zapata: *"We lost you/But not your message/Your courage/Your strength/ Your cause/Your struggle."*

And the message, the cause, of WriteGirl is also about courage and strength, the struggle to find yourself through writing. Keren Taylor, her staff and the mentors of WriteGirl enable teenage girls to enter their hearts and minds and souls and to write what they find there in bold ink.

Barbara Abercrombie
Author of *Writing out the Storm* and writing instructor, UCLA Extension
WriteGirl Advisory Board Member

introduction

Voices whisper, shout, giggle and cry out from these pages — the brave and bold voices of the women and girls of WriteGirl. It has been an honor for me to put this collection together and spend some time with these creative minds.

When the submissions started rolling in for this anthology, we were hoping we'd get the depth-charges that we hear at our monthly workshops. And we did. Much of the writing in this book came directly from an experiment at a mentoring session or WriteGirl workshop.

With more than seventy women and girls in one room, all focused on unlocking their own doors to creative self-expression, WriteGirl workshops are electric. My absolute favorite moment is when a girl stands, rather, springs up and shares with everyone something wonderful she just wrote, after having said, "I can't write anything" or "I don't have anything to say" only a few hours earlier. That's an instant change in perception and a powerful experience to take away and apply confidently to other situations that might start out with "I can't" or "I'm not." At the end of each workshop, everyone writes a *thread* — an anonymous comment on the day. You'll find these *threads* at the beginning of every chapter — they'll give you a glimpse of the inspiration and solace found in the word-world of WriteGirl.

There are stories behind all the stories you'll read here — complicated, multitextured, emotional backdrops to these pieces of mind. Like a photograph and the eye that captured the image, it is impossible to separate the art from the artist. And who'd want to? You'll get to know these WriteGirls as you read what they have to say and what they choose not to say.

It must be said that the publishing of this book isn't the end of something — it's only the beginning. Every woman and girl represented here has many more words to come. This is just a little of our bold ink.

Keren Taylor
WriteGirl founder and tear-duct champion

Silence is ok — it's a writing opportunity.

When you get in touch with your inner voice —
AND lose your fear of embarrassment and inner critic, amazing writing pours out.

THIS IS ME

Marlynne Carrera
Age 16

*One night
I was in
bed and I
was freezing
so I couldn't
sleep. I
wrote this
instead.*

frozen wings

i'm cold

that's all i can say

my wings are frozen

i can't seem

to be able to fly to

dreamland just yet

the wick of the candle

flickers

yet

no hay sol solo luna

luna de hielo

que no calienta

mi respuesta a tu pregunta

no se puede decir

en ninguna lengua

i'm cold

i'm young

i'm stupid

i'm brilliant

i'm unsure

i'm bold?

not really.

Jen Shiman
Mentor

drumming

one day
when i sit down and begin
— lock in —
i won't even think about what comes next,
i'll just know.

this is what joy feels like:
when intuition and desire
finally replace self-consciousness
and command my body.

even the possibility, the potential,
leaves me ecstatic.

Kioya Roneshia Cummings
Age 14

if you're not...

If you're not Kioya Roneshia Cummings

You don't know how much pain I feel

You don't know how many times I cry at night

You don't know what it's like to be confused inside.

You don't know how to deal with

friends putting pressure on you about doing drugs.

You can't truly understand why people come to me for advice

With attitudes even misconceived at times

When you try to be a decent friend

and your friends betray you

You can't know who I am and what I do

Until you walk one day in my shoes!

Romelyn Gutierrez
Age 16

walk

*You don't
know why
you can't
feel anything
else. Even
if dogs eat
you, you
still love.*

I walk the barren existence
sun beating down
sun beating down on me
pricklies speckle the land
as I walk straight and aimless
though they bury into me
I cannot feel it
for you have melted my mind
and numbed my skin
to the pain outside
keeping my agony deep within
the rays are high noon
and plummet, browning my skin
from chin to thigh to shin
mirages appear
my former fauna, flora,
the butterflies — that frighten me like the web makers
waterfalls, lakes, brooks
I do not thirst for kind sun
though my skin desiccates
I do not thirst
though my throat is parched
I walk on, now, towards the moon
ancient hounds howl, their yelping pups near
they smell my want of something
and cascade down the cliff
past the hill
closer, closer to me
and knock me down
maul at my viscera
I lie as the sun rises
to burn me once again
and in my mind I am walking,
still walking this barren existence.

Amaela T. Wiley
Mentor

poem at 29

The clock ticks like slow-grind music
I rock it out, wait for fate
Wonder what an incision to the back feels like,
A scalpel slicing flesh
Like my knife going into juicy red tomatoes
At no point since high school hormonal episodes
romanticized suicide in the
15-year-old mind of loneliness
have I contemplated life's end
The biopsy made death real
caused heartbeat to palpitate
       Asked:
       How many times have I been to the beach?
       Have I watched the tide come in enough?
Round midnight I wonder:
       Post mortem
       How many old slips of paper
       With pieces of my soul will they hold
       Making what sense they can of my
       Unfinished business?
I think about weddings
And funerals
And having no one to
Leave
       Behind
No birth to boast
And no hands to hold onto
Before I go under
It's the words, always the words
That send
Stomachs
       Tumbling
Because until they say
The Words
       There's nothing to be done
And the waiting
       Is
A sure thing

Gloria Espinoza
Age 17

untitled

Adulthood
is on my doorstep
Whispering the blessed
Word
Knocking in my eardrum
Wanting to get in.
Destroying this hell of life I live,
Leading me to the unknown.
Stepping on my fingernails as I crawl,
Pleading to be let go.
High stress
Low joy
Both
As gravity forces from opposite sides
Of the world.

23

Nancy Patricia Garcia
Age 19

We went
to MacArthur
Park where
there were Aztec
dancers, and
they have
an aroma
called "copal"
that they burn
to the north,
south, east
and west.

my color

My color is as beautiful as my eyes

My heart dances with the drums

Every time she sees the people dancing

Dancing for the rain to fall.

I love the sound of the wet floor

I stay there,

Having this emotion inside me

Feeling like a bird.

Lilit Matevosyan
Age 16

being an armenian

Being an Armenian is a pretty tough job. You've got to follow the
rules, and if you don't you're in trouble. As an Armenian, you've
got to marry an Armenian guy or girl, share the same celebrations
like April 24th, the Armenian Genocide, or March 8th, Mother's
Day. No matter where the Armenian people are around the globe,
they don't fall under other rules. They have their own customs and
traditions. Armenians are really hard people to get along with. I
am Armenian, and I love my culture's traditions, but sometimes,
they're annoying. But I enjoy following them.

Alli List
Age 12

i'm strapped in

I'm strapped in…

Stuck down to the rules
With so many thoughts
None of which can be
For my mind is black
With worry and distress
Rules are killing me

I'm strapped in…

Stuck in a structured plan
Pretending to be that
A creature you want
I'm not it

When you speak to me,
You're telling me that __
All that I am not…
Looking in the mirror
I'm not seeing
The same thing you see
That image, it's not me

I'm strapped in
Stuck in a structured plan
Pretending to be that
A creature you want
I'm not it

Jordyn Kruse
Age 12

untitled

Struggling to break the surface

Kicking hard with all of my might

Water fills my lungs as I gasp for air

All about me water

My strength is no match for the mighty sea

Still I struggle to reach the surface

Waves force me down

I try to yell for help but all that comes out is a stream of bubbles

Kicking paddling but, still drowning,

It's no use

So this is what it is like to know the end has come

This is the end

Treasured memories wash through me and I calm

I no longer struggle against the overpowering sea

I know I will not win this wrestling match

I allow myself to relax

Slowly I begin to sink down down down into the dark depths of the sea

And when all light seems to have vanished forever I see a glow of blinding white

Faces that I do not recognize yet I feel have always been watching me

Appear out of nowhere and smile in a reassuring manner

Their gentle hands take my own and guide me to the light of eternity

Then I know this is not the end it is merely the beginning

Keinesha Jackson
Age 16

*I wrote
this during
the Poetry
workshop.*

redwood

Slim like a fragile tree branch I stand

tall like a redwood tree.

Strong as a twenty-year-old tree bark.

Mood changes like the wind

blows the leaves, a friend to others

as we grow closer.

Grows with soil from loved ones.

Hard to be brought down

never going to be cut down.

I am a redwood tree.

Heather Duffy-Stone
Mentor
&
Marry Guerra
Age 15

a conversation between 15 and 25 (excerpt)

15: I think now I understand why people say, "Oh, she's in *that age*." I have analyzed the situations in which this happens and I think the reason for this (in part humiliating and belittling) comment is that going through the teenage years is about realizing a lot of things about life, its functions, and obstacles. You know, the whole "enlightenment" thing.

25: "That age," people say. Condescending. "That age," they say, because they don't remember or want to forget or never understood. This IS about obstacles. The obstacles are those who look down, from under their eyelids, from an exaggerated height that says *You know so little and I know so much*. It says *I'm twice your age and I know nothing about love so how can you*. But from here I know of a future I see and a present I live and it's my height that maybe they should be looking up at.

15: I just realized something — people write songs because they are confused. If they knew exactly what they were doing they wouldn't need to write. I think that's why I like to write, because I'm confused. A lot of it is about not having a road map to life when you're 25 (or 15).

25: For a little while, when we're learning to speak and walk and read, our parents are the map. But really, it's always you. And how do you build a map of roads you've never seen and destinations you can't imagine. It's the only way.

15: I wonder sometimes about the outcome of my choices. I'm not certain what I truly want, to be here, or there. I don't know if what I'm doing will leave me satisfied and I don't know if I'll regret this. I'm angry because I'm confused, angry and frustrated like I was when my favorite scarf blew off of me without me knowing. I feel like I've lost forever that feeling of comfort that I had in New York before I lost my scarf.

Heather: *This is an ongoing piece — a dialogue not necessarily between two people, but two ages, two stages in life, two similar minds with similar interests and worries.*

29

Mara Bochenek
Age 14

tee hee

I wear a tie people think
I'm a guy

I wear a skirt people think
I'm a girl

I lost my tie someone
Cut it off thinking
I was a guy

I put a pair of pants on
I got a little cold
They thought I was a girl

I put a leather tie on
With a long-sleeve pink shirt
And a pair of blue jeans.
HA-HA I WIN I GOT ALL THE GUYS

Chris Culler
Mentor
&
Susanna Samart
Age 17

love is pain

Love is pain...

... because Susanna writes it on her arm every day
  (and Chris can only hope that it isn't with indelible ink!).

... because a beautiful sunset is too big to embrace.

... because Susanna's best friend doesn't care about much
  (like almost nothing), but he cares about her.

...because love is stressful.

... because when Chris last hugged her grandfather,
  she didn't know that it would be for the last time.

... because Susanna's grandfather used to be so fun,
  but now he's so quiet because he's so old.

... because life is hard.

... because Susanna would like to kill the Khmer Rouge person who
  made the dent in her mother's head.

... because everyone has their own life to deal with.

... because Chris listens to hear her husband
  breathing in his sleep.

... because Susanna wonders who's going to be there
  for her in the future.

... because every hello also has a good-bye.

... because love and pain sometimes walk hand-in-hand.

Chris: *I saw at
one of the work-
shops that Susanna
had written "Love
is Pain" on her
arm, and so I
suggested that we
write a poem about
what it means to
both of us. I asked
her veiled questions
on note cards:
"Love is pain
because..." and
"My mother is
unique because..."
and "I hate war
because..." Out
of her answers,
her story emerged.*

31

Veronica Sandukhtyan
Age 15

ordinary day

It was the eve of Christmas, where I laughed with the sky

It blew its hand on my leg as it said "Hello,"

The prison fatigue was placed heavily next to me

Times when a jig was a mere embrace to be someone else

I smoked awhile setting the fresh cigar on the tip of my lips

So that I wouldn't disagree with its power the first time

And later took a swig of the Jack Daniel's whiskey I had saved up

The trees began to cry because I felt their leaves slop on my knees

Each a different color, each a different emotion

Kicked my shoes off and began to walk out in the street

No one was out though, probably at a party somewhere

Grass was darker than usual, but soft as well,

So I decided to rest awhile

Lying down, playing with the fringes of my black hair

Feeling as though each strand of my green sanctuary was sucking me down

The air began to grow with clarity and the clouds seemed to slowly retire

The moon was set in a chiaroscuro of blue light, full,

Not half-distorted like it usually was

It began to fall, it landed in my hand

I placed it in my pocket and stood up

Its clear glow was shining through my clothes

I could see it glaring in my suburban street

No sounds swiveled in the air, but this was normal

I did hear silence though

The streets began to flood, little rivers were flowing between my toes

It was quite cold, I could tell because the fish weren't in sight

Finding warmer rock they had fled

I kept walking, searching for something to do

I saw a priest displaying "Religion" for tonight, but I walked past him

It was getting pretty cold, the water was reaching my thighs now

I saw the fly in Man Ray's photograph fly toward me

I smashed it with my hair

I got tired, so I went back home

Where I slipped silently into my floating bed

Looked more like a boat, then I sailed away.

*These came out
of an experiment
from the
Journal Writing
workshop where
we were asked
to pull something
— anything —
out of our
pocketbook,
backpack or
pocket, and
write what it says
about us. At
first, it's just
a thing. And
then the thing
becomes
a story.*

Keren Taylor
Mentor

the collector

My bag is so heavy these days, I am a little afraid to reach inside. No telling what might attach itself to my hand. In the center divider, I pull out a bottle-stopper I had bought at a flea market in Quartzite, Arizona. It's an old stopper - mottled blue glass looking like it was dug up from somewhere in the desert. I bought it to fit on one of the old colored bottles that line my kitchen windowsill. It was only a buck. How can you go wrong for a buck?

I love bottles. And boxes. Containers in general. The world is so open. Amazing things grow on trees, sprout from the center of flowers, fall from the sky, fall out of pockets. Containers give you a chance to trap pieces of the world and hold them in your hand. Marbles. Dice. Seeds. Rice. Broken pottery. Fortune cookie fortunes. The beauty and magic of something ordinary is magnified when multiplied.

One lentil is not the same as a bin of tiny red lentils.
One river stone is not the same as a river full of soft smooth black rocks.
One bottle is not the same as a row of colored glass.
One reason is not the same as a million questions.

I'm a collector. I break the world down into bite-size fragments. I chew them over, feeling their textures inside my body. It's not easy to explain the lure of ball bearings in a wooden box, or cool mah jong tiles in my hand, or rusted bottle caps in a hollow bamboo stalk, but I cannot stop. I am collecting myself.

Pamela Becerra
Age 16

i wear the teeth

My friends and I decided to make a school night fun, so we all headed over to Shakey's. After crunching on a couple of pizzas, we decided to go and play the arcade games they had. So I went to cash my dollars for tokens. I knew I could only spend one dollar on games, so I carefully observed the games I wanted to play. I thought to myself, *"These are a bunch of kids' games."* But hey, all my other friends were enjoying them.

After wasting all my tokens, I decided to go exchange my tickets for a prize. I only had twenty-five tickets, so, as I looked at the prizes, I saw this pair of disgusting plastic bloody teeth. It was as if they were made especially for me. They were calling my name.

"I have to get them," I said to myself. I was just in luck. They were worth twenty-five tickets, exactly what I had.

As soon as I got a hold of them, it was laughs at school. My friends and I have this rap performance we do during lunch. For my act, I wear the teeth. It was so surprising what an impact this pair of cheap plastic teeth had on people and on me. These teeth say a lot about me. They show confidence. You're probably saying, "Why confidence?" Well, because I have the guts to wear them around school without thinking or caring about what people say. They other thing that they say about me is that I love to make people smile. As soon as I see a frown, I just pop in my handy dandy pair of teeth and bring a smile to someone's face. These teeth are like a disguise. They hide my fear of embarrassment.

I've carried these teeth in my purse for so long that when I put on my fake pair of teeth my mouth all of a sudden feels like a bouquet of wild blossoms. That's probably because I keep my body spray in my purse. So ironic that such an ugly thing can have such a beautiful taste.

You never know what you can find in your purse, or under your bed. But just remember, everything has a story behind it.

Glenda Garcia
Age 15

i was old enough

I was old enough to be disappointed by my abusive father.

I was old enough to see addiction around me.

I was old enough to be told the truth about Santa Claus when I was 5.

I was old enough to get the MTA when I was 8.

I was old enough to endure the act of fornication at the age of 14.

I was old enough to see my mom struggle trying to get ahead and always ending in the same spot.

I was old enough to realize I have never had faith.

I was old enough to confront my mother on my disbelief in God.

I was old enough to know that sex and drugs have no future.

I was old enough for plenty more but to this day I am in denial of.

Yet I am not old enough to be with the one I want, the one I have come to need.

Why?

Well, because I am old enough to be traumatized, but in society's standards I am not old enough to LOVE.

Ramona Jones
Mentor

*I wrote this
poem one day
while sitting
at home
really bored.*

greener pastures

What will my pasture bring?

Will it bear fruit for the spring?

Will it remain barren and still?

Or will there be growth and maturity?

Will I see lilies and fields of gold?

Or will I stay waiting, growing old?

Streams of life run down the riverbanks.

I try to catch up

but the meadows are too wide.

In this grandiose pasture

there is uncertainty.

I don't know what will happen,

I don't know what will be.

So I sit and lie in wait for my

greener pasture's duly fate.

In the Poetry
workshop,
we had to
use metaphors
while describing
parts of our
body.

Mariana Vásquez
Age 14

me

My eyes are like two

Shining stars far away

In the sky

Glowing with brightness

All the time.

My mouth connects

To them as it opens to

Laugh.

I smile all the time.

Like when I walk, it's as if

I see clowns everywhere.

Ivonne Cortez
Age 16

As a teenager,
it's hard to
develop your
own individuality
when you're
surrounded by
media and
propaganda
that is trying
to make
you change.

scared

Scared, that's who I am,

I am a young girl stuck in a trance

I think misconceptions make up this society

It's one of the things that makes it hard to look inside of me

I'm scared of living a life of loneliness

Because I find it rather hard to live in happiness

I'm scared of not succeeding in life and being perceived as a failure

I'm scared of loving or experiencing things I never did before

I'm scared of losing because what do losers bring?

I'm scared of winning because it might change into a brand new thing.

Whatever life brings my way

It's up to me to go or to stay

The road ahead past these teenage years is never easy

And I know it's a growing period in which I get to see

Who and what I choose to be

When and where I will be free

But for now I'll hold my fears

Well at least for a few more years...

39

Ivonne Cortez
Age 16

*I wrote this at
the Poetry
workshop,
where we used
all of our
senses in our
writing.*

senses

I am like the distressing girl worried about life

I see the world around me and hope that I will suffice

I feel like a soft silk cloth over a sand dune

I smell like that morning coffee dancing to a new tune

I hear my own insecurity like the sound of rock songs

And I taste like a freshly-out-of-the-packet Ding Dong.

Selene Gomez
Age 17

Wendy (Mentor):
*After I was
introduced to
Selene, she
began to describe
a difficult day
she'd had
recently. I asked
her to write
about it, and
she came up
with this.*

a fiend for freedom

I got caught up in the system, and now I can't get out. I feel like a stupid girl, who, by curiosity, went in a cave, a dark cave. I see shadows moving around me. I'm scared to make any move, so I try to stay still and calm, so anything in the cave won't hurt me. I don't even try to get out 'cause if I do, I know there's a big bear waiting for me. So I sit there all along waiting for somebody from outside to come and stretch out a hand and tell me, "It's OK. Come out. You can feel the warm welcome of freedom again." But then again, I'm just waiting for that day to come.

41

Since this program is just so great, I wonder when we are going to make WriteBOY!

A day that begins with trigonometry is destined to suck...until WriteGirl comes along and saves the day, gives some peace of mind and words to a numerically challenged girl like myself!

THIS IS US

Alma Castrejon
Age 17

to: zapata

I wish I had met you

A great man

With no fear

Risked his life for

Freedom and equality

You stood up to those

That killed and raped for no reason

You rebelled and did not

Give up until…

The day they killed you

—— the dirty government

That cut your life short

You fought and never

Showed weakness

What did it take them to stop you?

To silence you?

They cowardly killed you

Thinking that would end all

They were wrong…

We lost you

But not your message

Your courage

Your strength

Your cause

Your struggle

They silenced you

But

Forgot to cover their lies

Their arrogance

Their ignorance

They sent you to an early grave

But you never left

Not now

Never

You're still here

Fighting with us

With the ones that never give up, with the ones seeking

Justice

Equality

Freedom

Diana Rosen
Mentor

ennui

Quiet. So damn quiet. I flip

on the computer, test my Tetris skills:

yellow, blue, magenta tiles sprinkle

into the waiting jaws of the puzzle.

Maybe solitaire:

Cruel. Golf. Tut's Tomb.

I play them all, win them all.

Look at the answering machine,

its static red eye shouting its silence:

No calls. He didn't call. He'll never call.

Turn on email.

It takes so long, all the openings, closings.

YOU HAVE NO MAIL, it screams

YOU HAVE NO MAIL.

Go outside and check the real mailbox.

It yawns, spits out a stack of grocery flyers

and NO MAIL

He'll never write. Never call. Never come by again.

I walk the neighborhood for a familiar face,

but everyone is somewhere else,

doing something with someone else.

I try reading, but the poems

are too complicated, mysteries

too inane, the novels are not.

Do the girlie thing,

take a bubble bath, float away,

talk myself to sleep.

But, I talk too loud;

I keep myself awake.

Turn on the radio,

it crackles its tension in the air,

soothes not. I watch the light's

reflection on the water, stand

on the deck, give thanks for

the stars, moon, ducks, clean air.

Go back into my too quiet room,

fall into bed.

I sit up.

Something distracts;

The red eye is blinking.

Angela Martinez
Age 15

dream

I'm outside in the rain again
I'm just thinking away
I realize I don't like to be alone
to be alone

I wish to fly way up high
I wish to find someone that won't
break my heart

I dreamt of you last night
I saw you. I saw into your Spanish eyes
I finally found you
You're everything I've been searching for

My mind goes crazy
when you speak to me
with your soft voice so deeply

It feels rough to know you're a dream
I want you to be with me
but not everything is Hot Pink

I get butterflies
I wish to curl my fingers
around your dark night hair
I want to feel your soft lips

My mind goes crazy
when you speak to me
with your soft voice so deeply

I wish for us to be
Together forever
Together 4 ever
Together 4 ever

Maria Santa Cruz
Age 18

Maria Santa Cruz
Age 18

*This poem was
inspired by a good
friend of mine.
Sometimes
writing poetry
is difficult, but
this is one of my
favorite pieces.*

stranger

You're an amazing creature full of baffles and wonders
A rare person displaying an artificial façade for others
Always hiding behind superficial smiles and shallow laughter
Strange to your surroundings while struggling to live for others
You're always there for others without realizing all the troubles.

You're a human being full of crawling fear and confusion
Hiding thoughts and feelings, weaving into endless paths
Rough and blurry scenes to overcome in order to survive
Incarcerated emotions failing to escape every night and day
You're drowning in a pool of memories that bring you pain.

You never realized how hard it is to cope with life
Until the day you woke up and saw yourself entrapped
Wiping the ugly past and yearning for a fresh new life
Fighting and cursing this world of pain, but in the end
The hope of light is on its way to let you rest.

You, the stranger, have made me realize how lucky I am
To have someone like you in my every day
You're an amazing and beautiful friend who shared your love with me one day
I am grateful for everything I have, including you
And pray to God for every day that goes by.

Liliana Olivares-Perez
Mentor

*This is my reaction
to visiting my
severely ill
grandma on a
Sunday afternoon.
I felt so far
removed from
her...my
connection and
memories of her
are as a child.*

abuela

Generations apart, worlds apart yet de la misma sangre
The pale woman that lies there, a maze of tubes and needles
Is a stranger
Yellow eyed, incoherent, and thin

No te conosco

Donde esta esa mujer con las manos gordas y prietas?
Where's the dark thick woman whose fat, dark hands used to weave me
Tight, headache-inducing braids (a ten-year-old with a face-lift)?

"Me duelen Mama Quica, estan apretadas."

"Estate en paz chamaca, osi no se te van a desatar.
Pelo tan lacio."

Where's the woman who, when I visited in her Mexican domain, used
to wake me at the break of dawn with the smell of handmade tortillas?
My broomstick self, shivering in thin pajamas, tortilla in one hand,
stick of butter in the other.

"Hay, deja alli chamaca, te las vas a acabar todas."

My grandma, who smelled of sour milk and sweat. Abuela, who
converted every shoe into a slip-on, regardless if it was one or not.
Heels of shoes, flattened by her loaf-like feet.

Abuela, who used to embarrass me in my teen years.

"Mom, tell her to take off her dirty apron when we go shopping. Tell her not to take her money out of her bra."

Grandma who used to eat salad with her hands.

"I hope those people at the next table didn't see her."

Abuela, whose idea of a proper woman I never fulfilled, with my tomboy, aggressive ways. Abuela, as I sit here in my house, miles away, hours away, years away from where I began. I feel so detached, stranger to whom you were, a stranger in what were my beginnings. The struggles that let it be possible for me to sit here 32 years later and write about you, in a language you never knew, in a country you never liked, utilizing a skill you never acquired — in those backward days that you became a woman.

Abuela, I sit here because of you.

Abuela, who I never grew to fully appreciate, did more for me than I will ever know and more that you can ever imagine.

Michelle Semrad
Mentor

Inspired by my 4-year-old son, this is my first song ever!

wild everything

Shower, shave, my daily routines
Rushing out the door
Grabbing things
Grabbing you
In a hurry
While you soar
On child's wings
Always thinking what I got to do
Always forgetting that there's you
Pushing against me
Pushing against you
My belly big and round with you inside
Little did I know
We'd be holding each other up
You're my wild everything
Dancing on the bed
To the music in your head
You're my wild everything
Lucky ladybug
Ramone's inspired
Head banger
Frosty medleys
Kick me
Hit me
Push against me
Wake me up
You're my wild everything
Dancing on the bed
To the music in your head
You're my wild everything
Wild everything
Everything wild

Glenda Garcia
Age 15

dearest aunt

Before anything I just want to let you know I love you. Also, I think of you night and day because, although you are the sweetest person, I never want to be you.

The reason why I mention this is not to hurt you, but to wake you up. I can no longer stand how you feed that man's ego by putting yourself inferior to him. I can't go one more day knowing you're degrading yourself by letting him tell you that you are not good enough because you don't pay the bills, or letting yourself be offended by him telling you you've let yourself go.

I love you, but it's women like you who I fear the most. You are giving that man's ego power and letting your son have the most horrible role model he could ever have — a man who believes he could crawl under your skin and make you feel useless.

I honestly hope you take my plea into consideration and stop feeding that man's ego. I love you. Please wake up and believe that you will survive without him.

Always here,
Your loving niece

53

I wrote this on
the plane coming
back to L.A.
from my aunt's
bachelorette
party, held on
a tiny ranch
in Mexico.

Marlynne Carrera
Age 16

breaking the cycle

te oigo pero no te entiendo
what are you saying?
why did you receive 20 brooms at your bachelorette
party?
why did you get a
mop
a plancha
a duster
an apron
why?? is that all you'll be doing for the rest of your
life?
a slave to your husband?
is that what you're taught all your life to become?
is that what your mother became after saying i do?
is that all your daughter will ever be?
break the cycle of blind women
stand up and say no
return the gifts
demand respect from him
don't let him chain you down to your new house with
the duster at hand
buy yourself a crown and hold your head up high
for you are worth more than a few cleaning objects

Jennifer Gottesfeld
Age 17

*I had a fight
with a good
friend, and not
ready to speak
yet, I was afraid
to pick up
the phone.*

what if ?

The phone goes unanswered,
"You've reached the message machine of..."
Click.
Sneaking around the house as if you were an intruder,
Fearful, when you have done nothing wrong.
Ring, ring, ring,
Afraid to see who's on the other side.
"You've reached the message machine of..."
Click.
Unhappy, trapped, it's shining outside,
But the sun hasn't risen for days now.
The steps come closer and closer to your room,
You hold your breath,
Hoping they won't come in,
Sitting rigid and tall.
Ring, you look at the phone,
Ring, you wait for the footsteps,
Ring, wondering who is on the other end.
"You've reached the message mach..."
Click.
Typical.
Trying not to make a sound,
Sneaking to the kitchen to get a cup of water.
Sneaking back, hoping there is nothing on the way to encounter.
Ring, startled, the water spills,
Ring, look at the phone as if it were an enemy,
Ring, look at the phone as if it were your worst fear,
"You've..."
Click.
They don't wait to hear the rest anymore,
They already have it memorized.
Wondering who it is,
Maybe you should pick it up next time,
But what if...
No, just let it ring.

Tanaja Potts
Age 15

friendship

i always prayed to god that someday i could find someone who could understand me, someone to give me hope when everything seems destroyed, someone to carry me across when the roads get rough. someone to care so much that they could feel every tear that comes down my cheeks. god has answered my prayers. everyone of my dreams have come true, and no one could ever take away what god has given me — your friendship.

Kelly Castaneda
Age 17

*This piece,
inspired by my
ex-boyfriend's
ex-girlfriend,
is one of my
favorites.*

bird of paradise

Bird of Paradise
you no good flower
you popular flower
you high and mighty flower
you're the in-crowd flower
the flower that goes boom-ba-boom-boom
when trotting down the halls
the flower that craves every plant's attention
even my plant.

Bird of Paradise
you club freaker
you small shirt in 26 degree outside windy weather flower
you flower that shows no self-esteem
the typical flower that has to show off
you're the flower that every bad artist draws because
you're so easy
you're the flower that's a blur, when a plant opens
his eyes after a one-night stand.

Bird of Paradise
the flower that everyone picks
but to me you're the one who needs.

Lovely Umayam
Age 15

In using metaphors
to compare two
things that seem
so different,
I discovered that
they actually have
a lot in common.

boys 'n' books

Boys 'n' books …
Can never be together
No matter how hard you try
Of course, out of all the things
That are not meant to be together,
Boys 'n' books are strangely, curiously
Similar.

Similarity No. 1:
Some books are thick, some thin
Like the thick, burly jocks
Strutting around
And the thin, skinny, silent ones
Who almost say…
Nothing.

Similarity No. 2:
Don't judge a book by its cover
Same thing with guys
The handsome ones usually turn out
To be total __
The plain, brown bag wrappers?
You have to dig deep for color
And it's almost always worth the work.

Similarity No. 3:
There are mysterious boys
Complicated to read and figure out
They use hard, complex words of the heart
Some are easier to read…
Easy to manipulate,
You know how it will end.

Similarity No. 4:
Some books are confusing
With unexpected twists and turns
Like the mind of a player,
Trying to worm his way out of something
Confusing "his girl"
Some books are straight and to the point
Like a guy who blurts out anything
He wants to say.

Similarity No. 5
(and probably the major similarity):
A boring book with no sense of plot
Gets pushed away
But if it sticks around, on the table
You look at it and read it over and over
Like a boy who talks about something
On and on and on
That he wants to do
Even though it isn't interesting
He's always there, ready to be read
And love can grow
For that book
And that boy.

Princess Lucaj
Mentor

*I wrote this piece
for my older
brother, Tyko.
Though we
shared different
mothers, he
always made me
feel welcomed.*

tyko

I. Tyko

You found me
after my hair turned curly
          that Jewish kink from dad
a layover in Copenhagen
you flew from Stockholm
to meet my mother and me —
little sister you hadn't seen for 10 years
your gait from afar
sturdy
a grown angel
thick golden hair turned darker
wings embalmed behind green eyes
you sat next to me
mirage of life
more beautiful than I could stand
I, wild Indian girl
at war with poverty, prejudice, puberty
ravens scrapping, cawing under my skin
how could you be my brother?
minutes passed
lifelong impressions plastered like
wet leaves on naked bodies
we gazed at one another
through crisp soul windows
our deceased father lingering
somewhere between the two of us
we never needed words.

II. Neruda

after the new year
I discovered
you could not stay any longer
I pulled the Neruda book
you gave me for my 28th birthday
The Sea and The Bells
his poems — a healing tonic
of wind and saltwater
for all the questions you left us with
each bell's sound overwhelmed
by crashing waves
I kept listening for your voice.

III. Me

I awoke
to rustling wings
over ocean
misty sensation of peace
settling on swollen eyes
I felt myself, a woman
with hips, scars, and
many unwritten poems
stand up to the dawn
love simmering in my heart
I crouched close, close to shore
close enough for the sand
to witness
my departure from sorrow
— empty shell on a beach.

Glenda Garcia
Age 15

enter

The page said you cannot enter. Yet she, I, myself was allowed to wander through the pages. But she, I, myself was never forewarned of the consequences. How ignorant was she, I, myself to not see the prize was written all over, that prize was he, him, us.

Slowly he pushed her, she, me away. So close she, I, myself was to finally getting close to him, he, us. But my exit to him, he, us was easier to handle for him, he, us.

She, I, myself forcefully entered. She, I, myself was amazed by the emotions him, he, us brought.

She, her, my entering was prohibited. How foolish she, I, myself to forget such vital information and as expected she, I, myself was hurtfully pushed away and introduced to the back door where my, her, our exit would be less dramatic – inferior to all other endings in history.

Jackie Hernandez
Age 15

the day our lives changed

March 10, 1990: "Ya vengo mamita linda. Mami tiene que ir a trabajar!" My mother told me she had to go to work and that she would be back. Of course I expected her to come back. Each day at six o'clock I would get her slippers and run to the door. But this afternoon was different from all others. Six o'clock came, six-thirty, seven and still she didn't come. I waited and waited until it was so dark outside I could only see the stars bright. She never came. I cried and cried for many days. I wanted my mother. Well, could you blame me? I was three years old.

Later I learned that my mother had moved to the United States. Many people come here for a better life and it is true. It is really true. She came from El Salvador not having any family members here or friends to help her, but she wanted the best for me. When I was seven I was reunited with my mother once again here in Los Angeles.

63

The best times were the ones I spent with my mother. She has taught me all I know and I'm really proud of that. One thing I have learned over the few years of my life is that everywhere we go we see people who have a story like mine. Although mine is not complete, it is just enough to make you see that being an immigrant here in this blessed country is an honor and privilege. Now that I'm fifteen and here with my mother once again, I appreciate each moment that life has given me. Lastly, I'm proud to be a Salvadorian girl who is growing up and will become an FBI agent some day. (I'm a very big talker and I read and write and research, and I'm not very good with blood, but a detective would be great I think.)

Jeanine Daniels
Age 17

love is a gamble

Love is gamble
Love is a game
Boys get you pregnant
Girls get the blame

They say you're cute
They say you're fine
But once you're pregnant
They say it's not mine

They say they love you
You think it's true
But once you start to swell
They say the hell with you

30 minutes of pleasure
9 months of pain
Sitting in the hospital
Finally junior came

Love is sweet
Love is swell
But once you're pregnant
Love is hell.

Jennifer Repo
Mentor

bloom

This was inspired by the realization that writing can express in ways that other forms of language cannot.

He broke my heart. Plain and simple. I'd never been in love before. Sure, I'd dated, had boyfriends, each one professing to love me and me them. But this one was different. Slowly we entered each other's lives, unveiling our hearts to what lay before us. Someone once asked me how I knew it was love. I knew because I wanted to sacrifice and compromise for this man. The contentment of our relationship became more important than individual desires. But the red flags, blowing in the wind, were trying to catch my attention. I willfully turned my head, believing that love would conquer all. Take a chance, my heart cried out!

When a line was crossed, I realized I couldn't sacrifice myself, no matter how much I loved him. What was that line? Actually, it's irrelevant because the line is different for each of us, and it's what happens after that line has been crossed. A wise woman once wrote, "To offer the heart with full respect for the power of that offering means looking intently and carefully at where it is going." Why? Because to deliver love with our heart's energy is to offer our life's energy.

I let pain come, stay, sleep, and eat with me, never once asking it to leave before it was time. I think of him less now. I'm smiling more often. But perhaps the most important realization I've had is that, despite popular opinion about pain making you stronger, it's been the opposite. I feel more vulnerable, more exposed, and I think that's a good thing. In a world where we create barriers preventing others from getting to know the "real" us, this experience has opened up my heart even more. It's not the relationship that taught me how to open my heart, although it is part of the opening process. It's the willingness and faith to keep going that allows us to begin again. The heart is resilient. Just as a flower or tree bends and sways, so, too, can the heart.

Michelle Lewis
Mentor

*It has been
fascinating
to see the
connections
people make to
this song...for
some it's about
September 11th,
for others it's
an uplifting
pop song. No
one has any idea
what it was
about for me.*

any given day

I wish that I knew then
What I know right now
'Cause when I drove out,
I didn't think it would be our last goodbye
And if I had more time with him,
I know what we could talk about
It's a scene that keeps repeating over in my mind

So don't try to teach me anything
'Cause time is a circle spiraling out of our hands,

On any given day the world can change amazingly
On any given day we're face to face with sadness, hope and love
We have what we make of it, but we won't have forever
On any given day the world can change...

Took a walk through town,
Ended up by a highway
Looked miles up and down for anything to ease this ache inside
I'd stick my thumb straight out,
If I didn't have my family
It's funny how things you love and the things you dream collide...

Don't let go for anything
'Cause I don't feel like chancing it tonight, no

On any given day the world can change amazingly
On any given day we're face to face with sadness, hope and love
We have what we make of it, but we won't have forever
On any given day the world can change...

Amazing how the world can change each second you're alive
But you're the one who keeps me sane
You'll make everything fine, then everything is fine...

We'll have what we make of it, but we won't have forever
On any given day, the world can change...

Tiffany Cheng
Age 16

temptation

You sit there, so close
In actuality you're a mile away but
Your eyes feel so near, so warm, so inviting.

I know you're watching because I feel it
Goosebumps riding along my shoulders,
The very thought of your glare is intimidating.

You come over, slowly, gently caressing my cheek
And you whisper in my ear, pulling me toward you.

How I want to give in, it's hard
when I have another waiting back home.

Should I leave or should I stay?
The exotic music portrays my exact mind when I think of you.

Tempting, desirable, hypnotic
I struggle and fight with myself, debating whether I should succumb
or not.

Finally
I get up with a sly smile on my face and I ask
"How do you like your eggs in the morning?"

Anakaren Becerra
Age 13

chocolate chip cookies and orange juice

"Oh, Anakaren, you need to take a bath because you are going to work with me today," Mommy said. "And guess what? I bought you a nice blue dress."

I was so excited and put it on. It was beautiful! All different shades of blue in a pretty checkered pattern.

When we got in the car, Mommy kept asking me, "Are you excited to go to work with me?"

"Yes, Mommy, I love spending time with you."

We arrived at a big building that I didn't recognize, and when I looked around, I saw several girls my age wearing the exact same blue dress. I realized that I was about to go to school! I begged Mommy not to leave me. I was scared of being alone.

"Sooner or later, Anakaren, you have to go to school."

Mommy handed me a Pocahontas backpack with homemade chocolate chip cookies inside, then walked me into school.

I sat by myself in the cartoon room waiting for school to start. Then I spotted these two little girls sitting in the corner drinking orange juice. "Maybe they would like some cookies with their juice," I thought.

I got up from my chair and nervously introduced myself. "Hello, my name is Anakaren. What are your names?"

One of the girls said, "I'm Alicia, and this is Diane. We're cousins."

When I offered them some cookies, they offered me some orange juice. "Wow, they're really nice," I thought.

Alicia, Diane and I sat in the front row together eating and drinking while we watched cartoons. The teacher finally came in and called out my name, then Diane's and Alicia's. We were so excited — we were in the same classroom!

At the end of the day, Mommy arrived to pick me up. "How was your first day of school, Anakaren?" she asked.

I smiled and excitedly told her, "I made two new friends!" And Alicia and Diane are still my best friends to this day.

At the Journal
Writing
workshop, we
wrote freely
about memories
while ambient
and global music
played. I was
surprised to see
how music could
draw out
emotions and
memories that
had nearly been
forgotten.

Kim Purcell
Mentor

the bell

I remember my Oma and Opa's house. The quiet smells of the carpet and the air. The heat through the grand windows. Opa's cognac. I cried.

I failed my Opa. He was dying and it was two in the morning. I slept on the sofa; his deathbed was in the corner, a catheter in his hand. It had fallen off his penis and he couldn't go to the bathroom. He fumbled to put it on. His hands shook. It wasn't working. He rang the bell.

I slept. My dreams were not sad dreams. They were lazy, rolling dreams. I heard a distant chime like a church bell ringing through a sleepy town.

Opa tried to get out of bed. He grunted. My eyes flickered open. I saw his eyes, haunted with despair. He needed me or else he'd pee the bed.

My Opa with his big strong hands was dying. My Opa with his full belly laugh was dying. My Opa was dying while I slept.

Yaneth Prospero
Age 15

in the field

As he raises his face up

The sun's rays make him sweat.

Tired and angry he looks out at

The whole space with nothing

To gaze upon.

Both my mother and father live and work in Mexico, supporting the rest of my family from there. This poem is about my dad working hard for our future.

K. Lee
Mentor
&
R. Tan
Age 15

gotta let go

All of my life I've dreamt of you
Before you knew
Thoughts of a love that we would share
That we made true.

Now you're here in my life again…
Trying to claim the broken heart
That you have got to mend, but I…

Gotta let you go now, baby
So that my heart could love again
Gotta let you go now baby
Been holding on for too long and I got to let go.

You took my heart and held it tightly for me
But then again
How do I know that you still care
If you don't show me.

That I'm close to your heart
Even when we're apart
That I'm the only one
That you are thinking of, so I…

Time and time I've been giving you chances
But you never make up your mind
Stress me out with those one-word answers
Boy stop wastin' my time, my time.

Romelyn Gutierrez
Age 16

it

It is like some sweet
disease of the heart,
      That you, *you* have infected me with...
You, with your thick ways
You with your baby skin.

      It is like some fruitful poison
of which I have inadvertently taken.

      It flows through my veins
like milk and honey.

      I fall
down into a sea of warm waters
      I do not fight for long,
I let it take me.

      It is like a raw pain eating,
tearing away at my soul
You, with your blunt and tartly presence
You, with your gruffness

      It, Love.

73

Johana Perez-Medina
Age 15

i wonder

Ever since I laid eyes on you
I feel something I can't explain
But it's hurting my heart
With every breath I take.
Why I have this feeling,
I don't know
But every time I hear your name
It makes me want to turn around
I'm so shy
I can't look at your eyes
I cannot even smile
It makes me wonder
If you feel the same way
As I do
I'm so confused
But one thing's for sure
I'm starting to like you.

Kelly Castaneda
Age 17

This piece is about me and my mom, inspired by everything she has gone through with me.

strokes

Once again we're swimming through the fights and

screams, the fights and screams, and screams.

Don't you know we've gone through this already?

Don't you know I am tired of these same strokes we swim

through over, and over, and over?

Aren't you tired of the same strokes? Why don't you

open your fist brain and learn how to treat the world

of ladies.

Instead of beating them down like the wind

throwing down a falling leaf that's already been falling.

Lily Mendoza
Age 14

black

Black, tall and wonderful

like the person I care about

who always has a great sense of humor.

Black, unique and strong

like the way he walks every day

when he comes all happy and proud.

Black, loud and understandable

like the way he talks so perfect

that when he just opens his mouth

you can feel what he is saying.

Black, perfect and outstanding

like his personality is. He has a

personality that no one has or could have.

77

At WriteGirl, we write life. Boundaries don't exist. I feel free and powerful. The beings here amaze me.

THE VIEW FROM HERE

Yaneth Prospero
Age 15

I wrote this sitting at home, not knowing what to do, watching the time go by.

time

The time goes faster and faster and I'm here.

I can't even take a step. I close my eyes and

when I open them the time has gone again.

As the time goes faster, I have no time to

do anything.

The seconds go

and comes the minutes.

The hours come and the days too.

The weeks come

and also the months.

The months go and then comes the year.

The year goes and what comes next?

Well a new year comes and all these things

start over again.

Mariana Vásquez
Age 14

@9:56

*Sometimes my
apartment
building is very
noisy, and
I wish it was
quieter so
I could sleep.*

Outside & inside

At 9:56.

I could hear a man

Screaming at the TV.

A bird chirping for food

And a car honking on the street.

Lots of things going on

And nothing in me.

A mom yelling at her daughter

To get inside and sleep.

Some guyz on their skateboards

Trying to do tricks.

Two little girls laughing,

Laughing at their feet.

My mom watches a movie

And me, I'm just writing this

@9:56.

Diane Valencia
Age 15

After watching the movie Dead Poets Society, *I gained more respect for other types of writing. But still I yearn for the outrageous.*

explosive writing

Forget censorship! I don't mind mentees and mentors writing about the fulfilling joy of pets and favorite foods, but I want something more outrageous than yummy wummy matters or even typical overly melodramatic teenage problems. I want subjects that touch upon atrocities in society, hidden psycho desires, mayhem in human thought, destructive secrets about mankind, mutilating taboo subjects to the social order suppressed by parental and Victorian adult authorities. I want us to go beyond the line of subjects about the beach, fat cats and favorite foods. Instead, let us write about crude subjects. Let us expose society's phony mass media images of peer pressure, crap, Hollywood, sex, politics, violence and TV drug advertisement. We will write about things that mock the accepted pop-culture values of Britney Spears, so that our writing explodes, shattering the idealism of *Baby Sitters Club*, ushering in new revelations.

Gabriela Cardenas
Age 14

that flag

I hate
that flag
and all the people living under it
saluting their lives to freedom
finding none but still believing it's there.

I hate
those cars
driving past you in the freeway
with those flags
flying in the wind
those patriotic s.o.b. fools.

and I hate freedom
for not being real
for being taxes
and laws
and tapped phone calls.

I hate that flag.

I wrote this during a history class when we were given an assignment to write on something we feel strongly about. This was basically a free-write, and it just came out. (I don't really hate anybody, so don't take this personally!)

83

These are my
reflections on
migrants, people
who fight for the
chance to make a
living. It was
inspired by a
road sign on the
5 Freeway
warning drivers
to watch for
people crossing.

Rani Sahota-Hans
Mentor

migration

Their hips pitted against each other, grinding into the late evening cool. The insanity of the back and forth insisted upon them as they understood their purpose was grand. Supporting the top half, giving in to the bottom and visa versa when the other lost faith. Joined hands slipped to let go, only to feel the cold air breeze by and rejoin them, drying they stuck each to the other. Opening, their mouths become drenched with pollen, fertilized they move onward without the pleasure repetitively felt by the act. Weave once tight, fell off their legs giving up all its knotted ways. Twists over turns, dirt comes running to take their place, the two walkers oblivious to feeling the substitution, carry on. Sun bladed beside their eyes from its friendship with the sand, its plainness distracted from the ocean's vastness, almost able to compete. Backs becoming one with packs, the moisture attesting, hunch over assisting as one of the avidly oiled limbs avoiding the lights. They lay down on limits. So eagerly awaited the precious time does not step up to the prophesy and they lay wakeful, mindful. Heads fall, freeing them from the tumult of the footed world.

Alma Castrejon
Age 17

erased

In 1519 she was erased
Taken away from us
Taken forever
I have to get her back

In 1519
You came and conquered
My city
My people
Our land
Our lives
Our hope

Erased forever
From the face of the earth

Never to be recovered
Never to see the beauty
The beauty of the temples
Those
Majestic pyramids
Our culture
Never to be recovered

You
The cold-blooded
Cunning killer
Took our land
And destroyed
Her

Our
City
Tenochtitlan

85

Kimberly Mercado
Age 18

ready to vomit

It had been years since I'd thrown up. Kneeling over the low toilet bowl, I watched gall-tasting water being contracted from my stomach and splash into the already contaminated toilet. As my head lashed forward, I gurgled and choked — not on the warm, bitter liquid, but on the taste of my breath and my burning throat. Cold and unaware of what poisoned me, I watched. I watched with cloudy vision, my senses were blurred and sleeping. Trembling, I reached for a roll of toilet paper. I wiped all remnants of vomit from the sides of my lips and the tip of my chin, then stood in front of the cold sink and rinsed my sour mouth.

The poison killing me was gone. I was no longer weak and shivering, but revitalized...and hungry. I stood — on my feet, disgusted and angry — angry at the toxin that I thought was food. But now I know...it was poison.

"This is how we should be..." I firmly said, peering into the mirror.

Ready. Knowledgeable. Angry. To survive, we need to be ready. Ready to see our own reflection, ready to vomit the poison that kills us as a people. I opened my mouth and screamed into the mirror what I wished I could say to all of my people:

"Mexicans, Central Americans, Western Natives — it has been over 500 years since we've been strong enough to vomit...strong enough to stand on our feet without trembling...strong enough to see our reality without stained vision. We are kept cold...weak...blind. Unable to breathe, we suffocate, we starve.

"How can we live a life deficient of nutrients? We do not know of food — what is food? Where is our food? It has been stolen from us and replaced with venom. We do not know of air — it has been minimized and polluted. We wheeze as we walk, unaware that there is a way — and there was a time — that we breathed without wind being sucked from our mouths.

"We do not know of anything that matters. We are ignorant of our history, our identity, our land, our genius...and everything that brings us life — knowledge as a people. We are unaware of the noxious waste that lives in our bellies, sustained by biting our entrails, stabbing through our liver and thriving on our essence. Our life continues to be stolen.

"With knowledge and courage, we should ignite the air around us with the flare from our lungs: We are Nican Tlaca, Indigenous! We are not your slaves! We are not Hispanic! We are not Latino! Hispanics are from Spain! Our culture is not Spanish, it's Nican Tlaca! Latinos are Southern Europeans, descendants of Romans! We are descendants of the Olmeca, Zapoteca, the beautiful Maya, and the warrior Mexica! We are the descendants of 4,300 years of civilization on this land!

"We have our own identity, we have our own culture, and we will vomit the poison you have forced down our throats. We will vomit the ignorance you force us to repeat; we will vomit the self-hate and the 500-year-plus enslavement of our people, our land and our lives. We will see, breathe and live here, on our land, OUR land Anahuac, as a liberated people. We will vomit the poison that kills us. We will stand on our feet.

> We will stand...
> We will know...
> We will be ready...
> We will be free."

I imagined our people free from all enslavement. More beautiful than any dream, than any picture, than any tropical garden, I saw that this beautiful land belonged to us. We had control over our resources; we knew we were all wealthy in ancestry and culture, and we had an abundant knowledge of our identity and our history. I imagined increasingly more details, more color, I felt the ground, smelled the air, and used knowledge from books to grasp our pre-European lives — then abruptly — it stopped. I couldn't see anymore.

I awoke to a terrible reality. I let go of the sink and walked over to the toilet. I took a breath, looked down into stagnant waste and saw the poison floating... dead...cold...and ugly. Staring into the swampy vomit water, I said aloud: "If only our liberation was this simple." Then I slowly reached out my trembling hand to flush the toilet and watched everything that strained me to my knees in sickness swirl and moan in torment until it was completely gone.

This is a personal essay I wrote that appeared in the Washington Post *on Sunday, September 10, 2002.*

Kate Axelrod
Mentor

untitled

At First Avenue and 30th Street in New York is the Office of the Chief Medical Examiner, where the circa 1968 décor is itself decomposing. Nowhere is the reality, the graveness of *that day* more apparent than here. The walls seems to throb — saturated with the anguish of husbands and brothers, aunts and mothers, who came day after day with the hope of identifying the shadow of someone who once was.

Adjacent to that building, behind neighboring Bellevue Hospital, is an impermanent site known as Memorial Park. The location has been officially designated, according to a handout given to family members, as "the temporary resting place for victims of September 11th...a place of peace where many have come to pay their respects...a hallowed space where dignity reigns and a grieving nation honors its heroes."

Nicely said, but make no mistake, the description is a euphemism for a large white tent and 16 Mack trucks holding both identified and unidentified body parts.

It is June 2002, and I am there. Along with my 88-year-old grandmother, May, and her 88-year-old cousin, Matty, we have come because that's where Barry is. Matty's 55-year-old son was an executive at the Port Authority. His office was on the 63rd floor of Tower One. He died on Sept. 11.

Actually, all that's been recovered of him is his right humerus bone. It was identified as his because last year, Matty sent a swab of the inside of her mouth to the medical examiner's office, where her DNA was extracted from cells in the saliva. The marrow of Barry's found arm bone had been mined for its DNA. Both samples went into the computer, where they were matched.

Memorial Park is for families only. No press. No public. No photos. An appointment is required because it's a "working area," complete with buzzing refrigeration units, crackling ultraviolet bug zappers and the faint smell of something alien. When the victims' relatives are not around, the doors of those trucks are swung open and coroner's office personnel are in and out of red plastic bins, which encase the out-of-view truncated bodies.

We are accompanied into the tent by a chaplain, a funeral director and two psychologists. Each listening, comforting, being available. The handout guarantees that "there [is] no restriction of [the] resources for the identification of human remains...[our] effort will continue until we have exhausted the limits of science." So I take that to mean, for years into the future, men and women will toil with the shreds of mortality in those trucks.

And, to be honest, I wonder why. Just so some day, who knows when, they can call a woman whose husband worked at Cantor Fitzgerald and tell her they found a tibia? I know there is a spectrum of religious, emotional and psychological issues at play here, but out of the more than one thousand people still specifically unidentified, how will putting them back together in tiny pieces – or ultimately no pieces at all – help us fight terrorism and abolish atrocity? It's an exercise with a futile yield.

As traffic whizzes behind me on bordering FDR Drive, the mundane flow unaware that they're a pebble's throw from the house of calamity, I am thinking it is grievous how much more we now have to fear than fear itself.

Matty said she came here to "get closure." But at the end of our visit, she lamented, she didn't have it. I told her that maybe "closure" wasn't something you could ever expect to achieve when your child is murdered in such a colossal, monstrous, display of depravity. But what she had attained was the essence of bravery by being willing to come face to face with such shocking evidence that she had now seen it all.

Then Matty lights a yartzeit candle, a Jewish commemorative tradition, and places it on the steps to "his" trailer. We see that people have written on the sides of the trucks, and Matty says she'd like to do that, too.

So with a black Sharpie and a shaky hand Matty writes: "Dear Barry, This is not how I thought we would meet again. I can only hope that my love for you will sustain you and your love for me will sustain me. Love, Mom."

I am fascinated by forensics and what can be learned from a single strand of hair. But these lyrics are really about the limitations of science.

Keren Taylor
Mentor

dna

All lies leave traces

Truth now comes in a bottle
A vial of DNA from some small part of you
Left at the scene
Thousands of tiny bottles
Line the drawers of cabinets
Filling the space between the earth and sky
Filling the space around the reasons why

They've got a label for you
You can't hide
The bottle is you
Science doesn't lie

What do they know about me?
Am I the lines in my hand?
They think they know about me
But I can't be defined
By what I leave behind

All lies leave traces

The greatest brains are in bottles

Sliced paper thin

White coats search to find

The brilliance within

Thousands of tiny slices

Fill the drawers of cabinets

Filling the space between the earth and sky

Filling the space between the truth and a lie

They've got a label for you

You can't hide

The label is you

Science doesn't lie

What do they know about me?

Am I the colors that I wear?

They think they know about me

But I can't be defined

By what I leave behind

All lies leave traces

All lies leave traces

Lena Valencia
Age 16

train station echoes

I don't have time for this game
Dashing on and off the dismal subway
The rules never stayed the same
You rewrote them every day.

Told me you hated time
The clock's murderous hands
It was a subtle crime
Stealing life with each second that passed.

So without a glance at his watch
We'd wander aimlessly
Mining for time lost
In the bowels of this city.

We chased it through tracks underground
Riding somber Los Angeles trains
Though dark metal wheels echoed time's sound
We discovered the pursuit was in vain.

It was time we wanted to kill
And time we wanted to save
But time would never stay still
It beat you at your own game.

Marlynne Carrera
Age 16

freedom or money

Liliana (my mentor)
and I did a
"magazine cut-
out lottery,"
and we had
to write about
whatever words
we chose.

Free

Free to live the life you want

No boundaries

Or are there?

Walls are everywhere

Cameras are *everywhere*

People are just around the corner

Waiting to ask for money

Or show you a new credit card

With a low APR

Do you believe?

Are you free?

Or would you rather have the money?

Jennifer Gottesfeld
Age 17

I saw an incredible guitarist at the Promenade, and there was no one around him. He had a gig bag lying on the ground with a couple of dollars in it, and, as the wind began to blow, I could just imagine them all flying away.

at the promenade

He had sung at the Promenade for a year now. The tourists would stop for a second to watch him play his guitar; no one really paid much attention to him.

"Look, another guitarist," the locals would chuckle and point, "thinks he's so talented! Go take your gig and play it for some deaf people. I'm sure they'd appreciate it," they would yell at him as he played.

The truth was he wasn't much different from any other guitarist. He had resorted to street playing because it was the only thing he had left — his guitar, and his daughter. What worried him now was how he was going to raise her on the salary of charity.

He decided he was going to blow the crowd away, make them stop in their tracks. He would do it for his baby girl, so he could give her three good meals every day. He tucked her in and worked on his songs by candlelight. The electric company had turned off his power two months earlier because he hadn't paid the bill. He was afraid he'd never be able to.

Saturday came, and he went down to the Promenade, guitar in hand, ready for the money to begin pouring in. He unzipped his guitar bag and laid it out on the sidewalk for people to throw money into. He could already see it filled with green before the day was over. He threw the only dollar he had left into the bag for good luck and ran to get a chair for his daughter to sit in to watch her daddy's triumph.

Rain clouds were beginning to set in, but that had never stopped anyone from strolling down the Promenade. No matter how threatening the clouds were, it never rained in Los Angeles.

He put his guitar strap over his neck and slowly strummed the first chord. People turned their heads and stopped. Halfway through his song he had a congregation around him watching him play, standing hand-in-hand swaying to the music his fingers were creating.

The dollar multiplied and multiplied, and within an hour he had made more than he had ever made during his year playing on the Promenade.

Just like he had dreamed, people stopped in their tracks to listen to his music, and something about that music compelled them to dig their hands deep down into the depths of their pockets and contribute to this starving artist's collection of green.

A flash across the sky signaled the storm, and the plush and pregnant rain clouds burst open their gates, they poured their tears on the earth. Like water droplets, the crowd of awed spectators screamed and dispersed, and in a second they disappeared, into stores, into restaurants, back to their cars, to their homes, anywhere that they were safe from the cold, from the rain.

A rumble shook the ground and a gust of wind stampeded down the deserted Promenade, taking his bag full of generous contributions and blowing it away. The wet money was blown down the empty streets of the Promenade. Soaking and heartbroken, he chased and fumbled across the deserted sidewalks after the scattered and wet dollars. His daughter stood next to her chair and watched her father scramble down the Promenade. He chased each dollar, trying to scurry and capture every one before it was taken hostage by the wind. His tears added to the wetness saturating his face, screaming, he tried to grab the money as it was flung into the air like a leaf by the merciless wind.

He ran, scrambling, grabbing at the air, running and tripping, fumbling and falling over himself from the heaviness of his soaked clothes. He began to scream, trying to peel his wet earnings off the sidewalk floor. He began spinning like a lunatic, trying to find the money he had missed, where was it? Where had it flown to? Why was it hiding from him? He began running, trying to find it, screaming that it would not escape him. Now disoriented, he tried to figure out where he was.

He ran down the sidewalk, trying to find where his daughter's chair had been. In the distance it sat there, but she had gone. He ran with all his might to see the chair, to see her empty chair, and in his flight he stumbled and crashed, and his mortal head hit the cold concrete.

Bleeding from his head, clutching the soaked money, he slowly exhaled his last breath and opened his hand. Soon after, the clouds began to pass, and the Promenade was filled again with its lively and gregarious crowd, now entranced by a group of college breakdancers. Behind the crowd his daughter was jumping up to see, a man took her hand and led her to the front of the crowd so she could see the men dance. And no one cared about the fallen guitarist; they walked right by to see the new show.

This is from an ad hoc exercise with my mentor inspired by Man Ray self-portraits where little changes from picture to picture.

Diane Valencia
Age 15

good or bad

good or bad?
GUM
sweet blue and pink
and airy, fun chewing
and blow a bubble.
or
sticky glucose coming
to get your teeth,
cavity causing,
destroying dentures,
a pain when it sticks
to your hair.

good or bad?
DEATH
Escape to
sweet blue and pink
and airy, fun scaring
and peace in heaven.
or

bloody fleshed Grim Reaper coming
to get your soul
body molding,
destroying anatomy.
a pain when it sticks
through your heart.

good or bad?
BILL CLINTON

sweet blues and jazz
and swinging, fun sax player
peace with new and youth.
          or
media-oriented
sticky semen coming
to get your white house offices,
scandal causing,
destroying reputation.
a pain when it sticks
no attention on other worse things.

In 1993,
I traveled to
Somalia to make
a documentary.
This is an excerpt
from a memoir
I'm writing
about my
experiences
there.

Deborah Reber
Mentor

enter mogadishu

As our six-seater plane began its descent into Mogadishu, I looked out the side window for my first view of the Indian Ocean coastline. The water was a cool, clean indigo, crashing upon the shore with white bursts of charge. The ocean blurred into the blue sky with airy clouds on the horizon. There were no fishing boats bobbing along the waves, but rather U.S. aircraft carriers and warships dotted along the coast like dark intruders. I had heard that the waters were teeming with sharks, but I would find nothing. As Ricardo shot some footage of our approach, I scooted along the back and continued my voiceless gaze out the smudged plane window, my stomach knotted in fear and anticipation at the unknowns of entering a war zone.

I spied the Mogadishu Airport for the first time, gasping at the awesomeness of the military presence. The airport was now a base, lined with canvas tents, housing thousands of troops, tanks, humvees, aircraft, helicopters and trucks from a UN blend of countries. Military equipment took up every spare plot of sandy earth. I could almost feel the dryness and heat through the windows of the plane as we touched down, taxiing past a half-dozen huey helicopters. The military camp went on and on. It was obvious that, despite the fighting still going on in much of the city, the airport itself was secure.

I have footage of myself stepping down from the airplane, as Ricardo had hopped off first and started filming immediately. Now, as I look back at myself as a 23-year-old woman, my eyes well with tears. There's something about seeing that young woman, hair pulled back in a casual ponytail, stocked backpack resting on her shoulders, sunglasses perched on her face to protect from the harsh East African sun. Remembering her excitement and fear at the adventure she's about to embark on. Knowing what lies ahead of her. Wanting to reach out to the video monitor and comfort her. Tell her things work out. She's convinced the trip to Somalia was the start of traveling to faraway places, making films about hard-hitting issues, being a news journalist. I can see it in her eyes, how much she believes this is true. I can't tell her that I know it's not. It's a journey she must go through.

Anna Liu
Age 18

village thing

Before my mom went for a vacation in China, she asked me what I wanted. I told her that I'd think about it and tell her before she left. As she kissed everyone in my family goodbye, I handed her a list and told her that's what I wanted. She smiled and told me not to tell anyone else that she was going to buy me everything on my wish list because they would get jealous. I had asked for jewelry, clothes and much more. Wow! I couldn't wait until she came back.

When she did, she handed me a piece of unfinished wood and said that it was for my car. I then asked her what am I putting wood in my car for, and she had simply replied that it's a Chinese thing — for good luck. She said that this special type of wood, according to a village custom, is said to keep evil away and that I should hang this charm from the rearview mirror.

I then proceeded to display the piece of wood in the pit of my glove compartment. A friend of mine happened to find it and questioned me as to what it was. She had grown up in China and is in many ways much more "Chinese" than I'll ever be. Yet she had no clue about what seemed like a piece of scrap from my dad's carpenter work. I shrugged and said it's a "village" thing.

Keinesha Jackson
Age 16

I was fired
up to write
this at the
Persuasive
Writing
workshop.

a letter

Dear Mr. Romer,

I attend Hamilton High School and am very angry about the treatment
from the staff. Many teachers here, but especially Mr. __, have offended
many students and made them feel inferior. Mr. __ is a good teacher,
but he is really rude. He talks to students as if they were not civilized, as
if we were cavemen. This letter is not just about Mr. __. It is directed to
many teachers. This letter may not change anything, but many students
are being knocked down when they should be pumped up to achieve and
go farther in life. I speak for many students when I say school is hard, life
is hard. We should not have to come to a place where we are criticized
constantly. Instead, we should be encouraged to finish our schooling and
become successful in life.

Sincerely,
Keinesha Jackson

Erin Aycock
Heather Duffy-Stone
Marry Guerra
Corrie Siegel

On a Sunday morning at a coffee shop on Hollywood Boulevard, two mentees and their mentors gathered around a sun-bathed table and wrote these accordion poems. The poems were passed around, each writer seeing only the preceding line, and adding hers to build a larger piece.

accordion poem I

Blasting is pretty much what we've come to expect
Seems like a path we have to take
Into the mysterious trees whose black roots reach down nearly to the core of the earth
Where they feed and the thinner, smaller of them begin to grow and climb back to the surface
Creating gaps, discontinuing time
A broken clock ticks feverishly in the sky
Counting down the seconds until we meet
Knowing it will really only be a disappointment.

accordion poem II

Richard Harrison has a Sharper Image barking dog tape that plays when someone approaches his house
You can only approach by boat, by canoe across the moat and he WATCHES you from the window
With glass eyes that don't blink he WATCHES
Staring into white oblivion
Stepping back into dark shadows
The shadows that tease along the floorboards and doorways and window frames
Shadows that give the impression of the presence of another
A slight halo silences the gray hint of thought
And in the distance – the dog barks.

Lena Brooks
Age 14

Heather Hach
(mentor): *We
decided to write
stories about
a word selected
at random.*

clock radio

Skinny rainbows bounce off the pools of oil collecting in the parking lot. I walk toward the beige brick building and push the doors open. The light inside is dim, the air old. A faded banner announces that this is, indeed, the Goodwill Clearance Store. Cast-offs of Goodwill thrifts build mountains by the back walls. People hunch over bins of ancient clothes, picking through discarded wreckage of the '80s and '90s, donated lingerie stagnates in the corner. I move to a bin and begin sifting through it, jumping back after picking up a pair of stained men's underwear by mistake.

I'm not looking for anything in particular: a sweater, some pants, the fabric of time. Someone tosses a yellow pillow out of their way — it hits my arm. My brother's drooled-on pillow I don't mind, it's this nameless, faceless bacteria that bothers me.

I walk fast toward the door. I kick something. It skids and hits the wall. It's beautiful. I stare into its blinking 12:00, 12:00, 12:00.

"How much for the clock radio?" I ask the checkout guy in the white surgical mask (old lady junk strikes fear in the hearts of men).

"A dollar fifty," he replies.

I pay and leave, weave through oncoming traffic, nearly drop the clock radio, curse the SUV to my right, drive off into the sunset.

Devorah Servi
Mentor

war rages inside this pacifist (excerpt)

As the warm but forceful Santa Ana winds break branches, toss patio furniture and cast heavier planters into uncontrollable courses, war continues to rage inside this pacifist. I wonder what consequences more treacherous and unrelenting sandstorm winds might have, that blind soldiers and further endanger their defenseless accidental civilian targets.

Recently, helicopters seem to be circling over my home more often and closely than I wish. I rationalize that it's probably extra surveillance efforts or the LAPD pursuing increased crime because of the war's effects on the economy. I tell myself that no bombs will drop on me. I travel back in time and imagine the terror my beloved Papa must have experienced in Italy during WWII, when he had no protection from war other than the kindness of righteous non-Jews and sheer inner courage. I remember how, throughout my childhood, he ran to the window whenever low-flying planes passed overhead. War continues to rage in this pacifist as I imagine huddled Iraqi families, faces aglow and aghast as an obscene number of Tomahawk missiles threaten to shatter their lives.

My heart pounds from being startled by the Encino earthquake jolt. With war raging inside this pacifist, I ask, "Is God sending rumblings as a proxy for dissatisfaction with how we are treating all of creation?" My growing sense of the fragility of life fills me with an urgent longing to express love.

I close my eyes and pray that my love will travel on the wings of the winds, through the aftershocks of the quake and, in the light of the bombs, to wherever people need healing and the opening of their hearts.

Princess Lucaj
Mentor
&
Perla Melendez
Age 17

peace

Princess:
Perla and I
wrote this word
association
poem at a coffee
shop where we
like to meet.
We saw it as
an opportunity
to vent our
frustrations
about war.

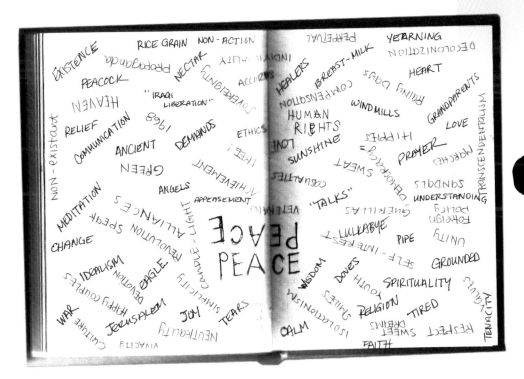

105

Diana Stamboulian
Age 18

*The title actually
took more
conscious effort
to craft, because
I wrote the piece
first, then figured
out a name for it.
I wrote this as an
expression of
thoughts that
I had collected in
silent reflection.*

the evil of avarice

On the basis of money and greed

Is our society installed upon a creed?

That of worshipping the dollar bill

Holds more power than human will.

Good men and women, alike chained

By money, mourn that their spirit is feigned.

And the man who gains prestige and wealth

Suffers from a loss of health.

With great fortune in his pocket (a toll?)

And none whatsoever in his soul,

Prices, paid to bargain his insecurity,

Hold no wealth that could match sincerity.

No amount can constitute love;

Money is left when traveling above;

Material possessions hold unnecessary weight;

So what will the rich man do when it is too late?

Try as he might to give up and fly 'way,

Money might hold him. In hell he will stray

And squander his solace in the thing his kind feed:

The eternal fire of capitalistic greed.

Diane Saltzberg
Mentor

avarice

Avarice/a twisted kiss:

Variant of the word Greed.

An acronym is what we need.

Recall Sins Seven, Deadly and Dire,

Imagine "PALE GAS" — *Pride* and *Anger* (play with fire) —

Continue with *Lust* (as flame attracts moth)

Envy, then *Gluttony*, *Avarice* and *Sloth*.

I was trying to write a companion piece for Diana's poem, The Evil of Avarice. *I don't have a lot of personal experience with Heaven and Hell, or God and the Devil, but I figured I could handle an acronym.*

Mona Gable
Mentor

a mother's journey to albania (excerpt)

His eyes, as always, told me everything. Pale green and luminous as colored glass, they were wet with tears. "I missed you, Mommy. So much." He was clutching a bouquet of pink carnations and a Mylar balloon that read, "Greatest Mom in the World." He'd worn his best shirt, a blue cloth oxford, and run gel through his sandy blond hair. I had on rumpled khakis and a T-shirt I'd been wearing the last 36 hours. All around us people in the international terminal at Los Angeles International Airport were smiling as if to say, "How sweet! The little boy reunited with his mother." I had my son back, but it was hard for me to rejoice. I had just come from a country where thousands of mothers would never see their sons again.

For ten days I'd been in Albania, writing about the work of an American medical team providing healthcare to the thousands of Kosovar refugees who'd been forced from their homeland in the spring of 1999. All volunteers, they had come to this tormented land hoping to exact some healing from suffering. I had come thinking I could be a witness to events, not get involved in people's lives. It was a notion I abandoned soon after we arrived.

```
```

Like many of the Albanian women I met, the mother I was interviewing had another son in the Kosovo Liberation Army. She had no idea if he was alive and was taking Valium for depression, a common opiate in the camps since antidepressant drugs were unavailable and, in any event, not practical because there was no refrigeration in the camps, nowhere to store medication. As we talked, dozens of women crowded around, occasionally interrupting to assist my Albanian translator. It was clear these women wanted me to understand exactly what had happened.

Many of the young Kosovar women reminded me of my nieces, with their poise and intelligence, their love of life. One, a slender girl of 22 with long brown hair and dressed in jeans, took my hand and guided me to her room, a concrete bunker she shared with her mother and six sisters and several relatives. The place was immaculate, with the family's belongings neatly organized in plastic bags hanging from pegs on the walls. After settling me in one of the room's two chairs, she made me Turkish coffee, serving it in demitasse cups. She did not speak English and I did not speak Albanian, but as we sat there sipping the strong black coffee and holding hands, it seemed to me that we were communicating.

```
` ` `
```

I recall sitting outside one humid afternoon with a housewife from Pristina, looking at photographs of her daughter's wedding. The bride, a pretty girl with dark wavy hair, was posed in a lush garden and dressed in a billowy white gown. When I asked this woman what she missed most about her home, which was now rubble, she smiled and did not hesitate. "My kitchen," she said. For the women, showing me their houses and scenes from their family life was not just a simple social gesture but an act of defiance. The Serbs may have stripped them of their identity papers, they were telling me, but they were not anonymous. Few of the refugees now had homes to go back to, of course, a reality many of them accepted with astonishing grace. One of the Kosovar nurses I grew close to, a sweet 23-year-old named Vjollca, learned this firsthand when a relative called the flat in Pristina she had shared with her boyfriend and parents, and a strange man answered. When the relative asked him who lived there, the man laughed and said, "I live here now," then hung up.

As I write this, I am sitting in my office at home, a place full of the odds and ends of a life. There's a big old sofa, photographs depicting various news events, chalk drawings made by my children, a framed college diploma. Books spill out from shelves everywhere. None of this stuff means much to anyone else; it means the world to me. Through a small paned window I can see the back of my house, a two-story California Craftsman that was built more than eighty years ago and that has survived floods and freeways and earthquakes, including the 1994 Northridge temblor that leveled good portions of the San Fernando Valley. I have lived in this house more than nine years now, seen my daughter take her first bold steps on its scuffed hardwood floors, seen my son evolve from making sketches of dinosaurs to scratching out algebra problems on the dining room table, and it would take an act of God to make me move out. As I sit here on this bright fall morning, more than three years after my visit to the refugee camps, I think of all the Kosovars who returned to their towns and villages only to find death and ashes and a grief I cannot even fathom, and how the fate of their husbands and sons may never be known.

Cecilia: *We were doing a quick exercise on how a subject can be described by creating similes and metaphors using the five senses. In this piece, So-Hee provided the metaphors and similes, and I pieced the poem together.*

Cecilia Hae-Jin Lee
Mentor
&
So-Hee Kim
Age 18

seoul

Seoul,
Although you spit me out,
There is no nostalgia
In my heart for you.

Your crowd of
Millions and millions
Run around like swarms of angry ants
Looked down upon by unforgiving gods.

Your car horns
Blare their complaints
All hours of the day
Squawking
Like a flock of irreverent blackbirds.

Your air hangs
Heavy in my lungs
Like smoggy vinegar
Forgotten in some giant jar
In the middle of nowhere.

You rub me raw
Like coarse sandpaper
Over already tender skin
Wanting for a cool balm of relief.

When I open my mouth
To protest,
All I taste is salty rain
On parched lips
Screaming for some sort of deliverance.

Seoul,
I don't miss you at all.

III

Today was very exciting because I got to meet my mentor. Also, all the activities were excellent. I laughed and met new girls. It's great to be in a place where we all share the same thing that we love – writing.

Here there's freshness and freedom to say what I want,
to giggle when it's funny,
to go into new places without first thinking – just writing,
just putting down on paper my purest thoughts – not just "correct" ones.

THIS INSPIRES ME

Clarissa Cisneros
Age 16

*I was waiting for
my mom to pick
me up after
school one day.
I was sitting on
the grass and it
was really
windy. I started
noticing all the
grass being
blown around
and wrote this as
I waited.*

grass

Free flowing,

Green with life,

Growing at a fast pace.

Swaying against the wind,

against the pressure of my feet,

against devitalizing weeds,

against the effects of time,

against the treatment

and the conditions

of its mother.

Fighting.

Living.

Drying up

and withering.

Grass.

Growing green

against the world.

Nicollette Barischoff
Age 17

This poem was inspired by last year's meteor shower.

under naked heaven

We wait
All breath and frozen fingers and coat sleeves
We wait
Staring through the black
The beating in our chests keeping time with the crickets.
While we steady ourselves for the shifting of Heaven,
Steady ourselves
And wait.

All at once,
The black falls away
Yielding to the whimsies of a beautiful God,
And all Heaven blisters and burns with a momentary brilliance.

A celestial torch
Burning hard, sharp furrows
Across the blackened veil of Night.
Temporary scars on the face of Naked Heaven.

The torch sails upward,
A heaven-worthy vessel
Taking a leaping soul up with it as it rides.

And then, the blackened veil restores itself
Making still a restless Heaven,
And ethereal splendor gives way
Leaving its tail behind
And falling fast under Naked Heaven
To be made new.

115

Trinity Gonzalez-Aird
Age 14

frida kahlo

An artist
A poet
A poet who sings
Through her colors,
Her shapes that
Come together.
Shapes that come
Together like words.
Like words in a song,
A song that soothes
That soothes her
Mind.
And mine as well.
Like words in a
Story that tell her
Life.
The story is the song
And the song is the
Paint that flows
On the canvas and
Makes a picture.
But it's more than
A picture.
It's a story
And
A song.

Diane Siegel
Mentor

This poem arose from a discussion about Frida Kahlo's choices in composing landscapes.

changing the horizon

Carlos calls it a psychological landscape
Her lying there on the dirt
the volcanic soil of Mexico
Where is the horizon?

Up high
all that earth below
It means security
She gave herself security with a hole in her chest
a neat rectangle of hollow air.

Now tell me
Where is the horizon?
Do you feel secure?
Is there just a little sky at the top of your canvas?
Are you grounded or
have your feet left the planet?

Are you flying in love?
Have you turned your neck impossibly to
kiss your beloved?
Where is the horizon?

Sliding blue on green
You can have your way with meaning
Keep it low or slip it away
Where is the horizon?

What does it mean?
Can you paint?
Do you think about the earth?
Where is the horizon?

If it is round don't worry
Your horse will carry you off
and one tree will grip the earth.

117

Cara Jones
Mentor

I wrote this song after an afternoon of swimming for hours in the wondrous sounds of Sarah McLachlan.

heaven's waiting

Why must I wait for love
Watching life pass before my eyes
Silent and proud, though I'm running out of time
Something is holding me
Turn a whimper into a sigh
Keeping me down on a bed of my design

But I hear voices calling to me...

CHORUS:
Ah, heaven's waiting for me here
Heaven's waiting for me
'Til I can touch the sky
With my feet on the ground, they tell me I can fly

But I can't wait much more
I taste the danger of slipping in
Into a womb, dark and comfortably cool
Wrapped tight in silk and wine
Wondering if I will ever know
Some peace of mind, and a love that's truly mine

Then I hear voices calling to me...
CHORUS

Winter is gaining ground
I know it's you that I'm waiting for
My eyes are shy and averted from the light
Here comes the avalanche
Flash of white and I'm underground
Seconds split time 'til I'm rescued from the ice

Then I hear voices calling to me...
CHORUS

Lisa Menaster
Age 18

I wrote this at one of the writing sessions with my mentor.

dangerous

It's raining too hard

Thunder sounds

And lightening crashes

I walk outside

I hold my hands

Out and open

I stick out my tongue

Drops of water

Drip off my tongue

Then it begins to hail

It hurts

But I stay

And let the hard

Hail hurt me

It feels good.

This poem uses
metaphors
to equate the
senses of
something from
nature to the
senses of people.

Lovely Umayam
Age 15

hawk flies by

The wings of the hawk, spread wide, up high
Looking down on inferiors as he flies by
Underneath the scepter of his mighty wings
Insistent with the high-pitched note that he sings.

The wind and the trees obey his commands
He mocks the sea and the sweep of the land
Morning, night, noon or dawn
He sweeps low over lakes and then he is gone.

His black tinted eyes, embroidered with yellow streaks
Keep watch as he swoons over rivers and peaks
But, alas, a deafening rumble erupts from the ground
A bullet flies through the air, mighty hawk is shot down.

Down, down, toward the world that he rules
His last memory is pure, of a world that is cruel
The wings of the hawk, spread wide, up high
Looking down on inferiors as he flies by.

Allison Deegan
Mentor

hummingbird and hawk

She is endless energy
Whirling, buzzing from tree to tree
Leaving stories, absorbing light
Learning morning, noon and night.

A hummingbird that shines and glows
A heart so pure, a mind that knows
A purple youth, still growing strong
Inviting all to fly along.

Up in the sky, with wings spread wide
Dark feathers catch the wind and glide
A little closer, making sure all's well
Patrolling between heaven and hell.

She is the hawk, her eyes see all
She will not ever let you fall
If you turn torpid, she'll be warm
If you fear rain, she'll stop the storm.

The hawk calls to the hummingbird
No need to wonder if she's heard
With different songs, birds of a feather
Have found a way to sing together.

One has wisdom, one has vim
One knows history, one knows whim
Evolving with each note they share
Flying through brisk city air.

Their nature cannot be contained in cages
Their music is the story of the ages.

This piece was inspired by Lovely's poem, Hawk Flies By, and the idea that the most powerful beings in nature are oblivious to our intrusive presence until we strike out at them. I am drawn to ponder how Lovely and I have managed to forge such a close relationship — me, a somewhat cynical writer, sometimes lacking in inspiration, and her, an energetic teenager who is curious about everything and smarter than I ever remember feeling.

Lori Obregon
Mentor

untitled

Pines frame granite crests
Wind whispers across the ridge
The sun warms my back

Brilliant blue, boundless
Sky – A canopy above
An insect clicks past

Twin Pine Poles reach up
Chiseled granite looms behind
Hair flies in my face!

I love the pine trees.
Evergreen, reaching to God.
Their scent fills my nose.

Marlynne Carrera
Age 16

Marlynne Carrera
Age 16

mi aleph

it's funny how

one day you see things

one way

and the next...well

different point of view

no one understands

as if the world has collapsed

and made itself over

into a ball of yarn

yarn of no specific color

an aleph of the universe

the escape of all reality

that suddenly stops

and shows its monstrosity

everyone's afraid of the truth

no one can look away

they try but

the bond

between man and universe

is impenetrable

a chain made with unbreakable links.

I was reading El Aleph written by Jorge Luis Borjes, and it inspired this piece. "Aleph" is the first letter of the Hebrew alphabet, and the Cabalists believe that the whole universe can be viewed through this mystical letter.

123

These are my
reflections
on seeing the
Dorothea Lange
exhibit at the
Getty Museum.
It was interesting
to get inside
the mind of a
homeless woman
during the
Depression.

Perla Melendez
Age 17

sunday dress

She was living under the bridge
Wearing her best clothes
Which were her only clothes, really
Which were her Sunday clothes
Or, what used to be her Sunday clothes
Back when there were still Sundays
Back when days had importance
When she'd used pain as an excuse
Before it became truth
Filled her eyes
Her face with creases
Of all kinds
There were lines
All
Over the place
Gave in
And even her
Smile refused to sparkle.

She was living
Dashboard belongings
Under the bridge
Corroded jewelry hanging out
Of the glove compartment
Charlie, Sandra, Billie
Toppled over one another in the
Back seat, wrestling the weariness
For sleep
For liveliness

As she did in her own mind
When she slept
With the moths picking at her sweater
And the fleas gnawing on her goose bumps
When she slept
She fell halfway into a dream
And woke up every day
Including Sundays
Eyes sweating tears because
This was a nightmare
And she wasn't sure
Of how long she'd be
Wearing her Sunday dress
All seven days of the week.

To her, Sunday held no meaning
It was a day
Just like any other
There was no telling
When the Depression would end.
The whole world was losing touch,
There was really no use
In beginnings and endings
Not even for days of the week
Because Sunday
Failed to bring that well-needed close
To the dust bowl
She was swimming in.

Jessica Emerson-Fleming
Mentor

*As I was driving
home from work
one day, there
was this fantastic
harvest moon
in the sky, but
since it was still
fairly early the
moon was low.
I kept losing
sight of it behind
buildings and
trees, and nearly
got into an
accident craning
my neck to look
for it because
I was so
entranced.*

moon hunting

Fresh bend of black
a blur between the buildings
A reason to pass

Here glint
there glow
An urge to discover
the canyons and crevices
of a stranger

The mystery of a disappearing act
like a shot of adrenaline
The light rises and falls
quick breath, until
the Harvest weights the sky suddenly

Then, with a glance behind, is gone again.

Jessica Emerson-Fleming
Mentor

southland winter

The burst of autumn in winter
burns my retinas
It's clear enough to breathe
today
And my thoughts turn
as ever in clarity
to unnamed colors that would
better remain dormant
Skin and fountains
Leaves trickling to the ocean
The shape of a mouth
I do not yet know

Artless rooms smell familiar
faint and citrus and
full of man
So that I can't help
but wonder
How much is known
How many
were there

How many leaves will fall
before spring dawns on L.A.?

127

Cynthia Harrington
Mentor

the first skydive

The sun is so bright it blinds that day of the first jump. The air tingles on your skin. Today is the day your body leaves the seeming safety of the plane and flies freely.

First you learn. In a classroom just like any classroom, the instructor describes how you will put on your parachute, how you will open the chute, and how you direct the opened chute to land you softly back on earth. You practice all the maneuvers. You look forward to lunch.

The drop zone activity cycles like a ballroom dance. The plane lands. The line of jumpers extends to the plane and disappears into the opening. The plane takes off. Those jumpers float to earth under pillows of neon pink, blaze fuchsia and white stripes.

The plane lands. The new load embarks. The plane roars back into the sky. Midway through the tuna sandwich, your name and your new best friends' names blare out over the tarmac. It's time.

You settle the straps of the parachute pack over your shoulders and tighten the chest strap and then the leg straps tight, yes, very tight. You enter the dance in the line of jumpers running to the plane. Once inside, you take the open place on the benches attached to the sides and running the length of the plane. The smell of aviation fuel fills the cabin through the doorless opening as the engine gathers power. You feel the lift of the wings and the wheels lose contact and the plane climbs. Experienced jumpers relax, some sleeping, some bobbing their heads to the music.

The dial on your altimeter advances around the circle, 3000, 6000, 8000. Jake wakes up and checks his parachute straps. Next to him Valerie quits singing and intently polishes the plastic goggles that had been loosely hanging from the chest strap on her pack. Up and down jumpers secure helmets and fasten chinstraps. One by one they stand and you stand. When the bench is empty someone flips it up against the wall. You remind yourself to keep breathing. You are going first.

The lead instructor maneuvers himself out the door, clinging spider-like to the plane's skin. Your other instructor grips the side of your pack tightly. You look down and see the toes of your boots silhouetted against the hazy checkerboard cornfields below. There's a tug on your pack. One, you rock out together, two, you rock back in together, three, your feet lose their grip and you jump.

You feel supported on the column of air, you see both instructors grinning at you over your outstretched arms. Like a bird, you fly. No metal surrounding you, no engine powering you. Just you, in the canvas jumpsuit and your protective headgear, flying through the air. Free.

So-Hee Kim
Age 18

*I think most
people can
feel snow
by reading
this piece.*

snow

It's snowing. Everything changes its clothes to white. When it touches your face, you feel cold and cool. It's snowing. You can smell fresh, cold air. Sometimes, its smell contains your city and life. It's light and small. You can't see it exactly, just think it is like a circle. Most people draw it as circles. Many circles are falling from the sky, making people feel happy. When you walk on the snow, you can hear the snow's sound, like when you bite a fresh apple once. When it touches your tongue, it makes your teeth cool. It doesn't have any taste, but sometimes it tastes like ice cream — sweet and cold. Sometimes, it looks like a cloud, cotton or soft quilt. When snow hides everything, I think a cloud is going down to the ground to cover everything. It is another sky. It is beautiful and I forget it is cold.

I am so excited about WriteGirl.
Anytime I'm feeling down I remind myself that I am a part of something powerful and great.

It's tough to find places where words come this easily.

GREAT ESCAPES

Nicollette Barischoff
Age 17

This piece was inspired by a true incident that happened when I was four.

drunk

Says the old man, sitting like bronze on the park bench:
"When did you first know you were white?"
"What do you mean?" says me,
"I've always been white."
"And I have always been black" says he,
and strokes the white hair on his chin.
"I'll tell you, child, how I knew I was black.
I was young once, once, child, like you."
I don't believe him.
"I was young once," says he. "I learned, though.
I learned about colors, child.
I learned I was black.
I learned the day I came home from school and asked
'Mama, what's a nigger?'"
Old man like bronze on a park bench.
"Mama, why do we say nigger?"

Clarissa Cisneros
Age 16

breaking barriers

Xochitl saw the way her father treated her mother and didn't know how to confront a man of male tradition in order to overcome town corruption. At 15, she saw the way town people approached situations of corruption and female intervention in situations of grand importance.

"How can I do what I know is right without breaking a barrier I hold with my father?"

Seeing her own mother face the hardships of male dominance in their home made Xochitl's stomach tighten as a wave of frustration filled her soul. Fifteen years of mastering a girl's place in society and the home were worthless to her. She had to reach out to her dad, but the newspaper held in front of him formed a wall she wasn't sure how to overcome. Her father read an article titled "Woman Rebukes Adulterer" with an indignant tone that sparked Xochitl's fire for what she knew as just and true.

Challenging every ounce of authority her father held, Xochitl snatched the newspaper from her father's hands and tore it in half. "I won't let you scorn the actions of women that do what I only wish I could do."

With that, her dad sat back with awe and disbelief.

At a session with my mentor, she brought in some fables from different cultures and read them to me. We then wrote our own fable. I wanted to write about a girl who rebels against what is expected of her. It parallels my own experience.

135

Pat Payne
Mentor

*I wrote this
from a photo
of a family,
with what
looked like
the father
hovering in the
background,
slightly faded.
He looked
like a ghost.*

spectre in the photograph

This picture of Alberto and his family was taken at an important juncture of his altered life. If you look into his eyes, you can detect a little sadness lingering beneath his ephemeral lashes. It is the twin's fifth birthday. Veronica, Albertito and their prima Consuelo are enjoying the celebration with wild abandon, playing with the confetti released by the exploding piñata. His dilemma? The camera is a Polaroid and the photographer, his beloved mother, fainted when she saw his image, his arm so clearly hugging his wife. (Postscript: Alberto's spirit, afraid of being discovered, turns into a bird, and arranges to be "found" by his children. The bird is passed from family member to family member, and outlives them all.)

Cheryl Klein
Mentor

*In the Fiction
workshop,
I wrote about a
picture of an
elderly woman
holding a
black-and-
white photo of
an old man.
My first instinct
was that she
was mourning
her dead
husband, blah,
blah, blah.
Then I thought,
'Who says he's
her husband?'*

old woman with photo

This is Eugenia. The man in the photo in her lap is Charles. She lives in West L.A. in one of those vaguely Spanish storybook cottages. She fits the neighborhood now that her hands have grown knotted, her sweaters pink and sequined, but there's no way she could afford this neat jewel of a house in today's market.

In her day — and there are so many odd reminders that this is not her day; the giant cars and tiny electronics — in her day she was a photographer. Good black-and-white stuff where the lines on her subjects' faces told of wars and loss and birthdays. Though she should never have been allowed to frame her own work. Her sense of style ended at the edge of the lens.

Her son gave her a digital camera for Christmas, and on the surface it seemed like a good gift, the way that on the surface her son seemed like a good son. Eugenia knew he was proud of himself for not buying her flowers or a bathrobe. Standing in a sea of wrapping paper, he watched as she fumbled with the tiny buttons and squinted into the screen — the would-be subjects of her photos already a movie, even before she took the picture — and she knew he was thinking she was confused by it. The camera sits quiet and silver on her dark wood dresser, a reminder that the world will outlive her. It was not confusion, just arthritis and analog nostalgia.

137

She remembers her thumb on the metal lever that wound her first camera.

All there is now is space: screen, camera, son.

Chair, window, Westwood — with the Persian markets she'd like to try if she didn't have to rely on that home delivery service.

The man in the photo in her lap is old, was old when she took the photo down at the harbor, her skirt clamoring for attention in the wind. Seventy-ish plus forty years of space equals dead. The grocery delivery girl probably thinks he's her husband, that there is no difference between the ancient dead and the recent, this old lady and that one.

Michelle Lewis
Mentor

Alli and I
decided to
write about
someone
opposite from
ourselves and
write about
that person in
a familiar
setting. For this
piece, we each
wrote about
our characters
getting up
on a Monday
morning.

michelle's experiment

· Male
· 48
· Prison Guard
· Ossining, New York in late Fall
· Name – Roger Gentry

Roger sat up straight in his bed screaming, "No! Get Back!" He caught his breath…waited to hear something…nothing. Thank God, he was only dreaming. Now he was awake. 5:55 in the morning. The static-y news station wouldn't start blaring for another 15 minutes. But he couldn't fall back to sleep now. Lola rolled over and mumbled into her arm, "What's wrong, honey, is it the dogs again?" Roger couldn't answer — his heart was still in his throat.

Exhaling loudly, he pivoted sideways and placed his feet on the floor. Mmmm, better. But could he stand? He wasn't sure. The dogs had torn up his left leg pretty badly. Oily black scabs were forming over the deep puncture wounds on his left ankle, calf and thigh. The rabies shots still made him queasy.

He grabbed the cane leaning against the wall and hobbled to the bathroom. It was still dark out. The sudden light in the bathroom felt physically painful, yet comforting, because it took him farther away from sleep…he felt the sting of cold water on his face. How could he go back there?

alli's experiment

- Male
- 64 years old
- Carpenter
- Alaska in the summer
- Name – Joe Beluggi

When I got myself outta my bed, the ol' floor creak-ed up like a bad habit. First thing I did was take myself out to Johnathon Spitter's fancy new har'wood store to buy a nice set o' oak planks. As my trusty ol' truck made its own way over the bumpy roads, I heard the planks jigglin' 'round in the back. Soon after I got me back to the house, I started to sand down the planks. And I tell ya, there ain't nottin' better than the smell o' newly sanded pinewood. At about ele'en o'clock I spotted where the sun was in the big, blue Alaska sky and reckoned I should get to makin' my lunch…so I put a pot on the ol' stove and poured some stew into it. Then I brought myself out to the workshop to make the chairs that Miz Golantshir ordered up jus' last week. My weary ol' bones set themselves right at workin' up a bit of a sweat, when I decided to check the stew. Seeing as it wasn't done at this here point, I went back outside to finish up my job. After a while, I bet to all who was watchin' that the suppa was goin' ta be done. I checked my clockwatch and went back to me kitchen and set the table. Mrs. Woodbine came down the stairs a-sayin' that she smelt some man cookin', and why hadn't I called her down to make some worthy food? Well, to that I replied, "Ma'am, if I had asked you, you would have told me to get back to work and stop botherin' ya…"

139

This is an excerpt from a novel I'm writing. This focuses much more on the mother, who is starting to become the main character. It's sort of the mother's "coming of age" through her daughter's eyes.

Alli List
Age 12

anadita's blond roots

Aunt Reesie and someone I had never seen before were on the doorstep, kissing, practically making out. Father gasped. It was a small sound, but I knew it was more of a pretentious "what the ___?" than an exhale of breath. Hakim Ahmed would never mutter an obscenity…no…he was too much the good man. So a gasp was his preference.

"My dear," he tried to continue as if nothing had happened, "Fa-la-la-la-la-la-la!"

Ha! Those words and songs mean nothing to me. I hear "Merry Christmas" and can't reply. All of my friends go on and on about their soon-to-be presents and games, while I sit and dutifully study the Koran. These people obsess over candy and Santa, and then they look at me as if I'm weird, as if I'm one of those freaks who loves religion, even though in one of the old countries I would be considered blasphemous. And then, at lunch, I pretend I'm not hungry while I sit and talk with my friends, trying not to stare at their food, 'cause that would make me even weirder, right?

I'm so tired from getting up at four o'clock every morning for the past week that I'm dozing off into alternate dimensions. Off in the distance (which is only about two feet away), I hear Shawna talking in jibberish, something about me and a party with some other people.

"Whoa, whoa, whoa! Take a step back and start with the first set of blah, blah, blahs! I heard like, three things you just said," I told her sleepily. Then she goes into typical Shawna overdrive, practically spelling it out for me. Well, more than practically, literally.

"Violett is having a party, P-A-R-T-Y on the eighteenth, one-eight. Christmas shin-dig, not your preferred style, but fun nonetheless. Everyone, and I mean, EVERYONE, is gonna be there! Randy, Justin, Bailey, Stephenie, Emile, Aimee, Jackson, Rhonda, Darren, Marla, Jere, Harrison, Julia, all of the normal 'us.'"

I sigh deeply.

I walked home veeeerrrry slowly, thinking about all the possible ways to tell my parents about this important, no…crucial party. I decided that my mother would be the best way in. At least, she understood. My father would be another story.

Mother was at the stove, so I went into the kitchen, grabbed a stalk of celery and nonchalantly started cutting. In my head, I made the tactical decision to tell her AFTER she had eaten...she'd be in a much better mood. Then again, who wouldn't? I moved the plates and silverware onto the table and noticed that it was the good china...the kind for company.

"Mother, this is the nice stuff...are we having guests for dinner?" I asked, watching how she tensed up at the words "mother," "guests" and "nice." Then she spoke, her blond hair falling down over her face, making her look like she did in the pictures at Grandma's house, before she was a Muslim.

"No, it's nothing special...it's only my sister and her new husband coming for dinner. And I just thought it would be nice for your father if we looked and felt nice, for a change."

"Aunt Reesie is coming? I missed her when she was gone on her tour of Europe! When did she get married? You never told me about it! Where was it? Who is he?" My mom (and I can only call her that when she's having a non-Muslim moment) sat down and told me the shocking news. "I never told you because I didn't want you to get...hurt. We weren't able to go to her wedding because Hakim would never allow it. It was too Christian, he said, not welcoming to us or our people. I tried to get him to come around, but he wouldn't, so I decided not to upset you with it."

141

Then my mom did something she rarely ever does...she looked straight at me. I saw why father fell in love with her before he could speak enough English to tell her his name. Her eyes were deep, as if she were an ancient princess, locked up in the figure of a mother/wife. This was the girl who I had been told stories about in the precious few times I had been allowed to spend with my Grandma Julia. The girl who had a brain with enough wrinkles to be Einstein. The woman with as much beauty as Jackie Onassis, the person with the grace of a figure skater, in mid-spin. I wanted to be just like her. But I couldn't. And I saw what was holding us in, my father and his faith.

So, I did something that shocked us both — I talked to her, as a person. "Mom?" and she sat up, startled..."Mom, do you ever regret it? Becoming a Muslim? Father made you... he makes you do everything, doesn't he?"

And THEN, she shocked me even more by answering. "I DID love your father, but, he couldn't love me...I was a Christian. And the Muslim religion had always interested me," she said, sighing.

"I was young and I didn't realize how long forever would be. Seventeen years have lessened my love, made it miniscule...I have had to watch my daughter, in whom I see the same love of life that I once had, be pressured into perfection, living the strictest of lives. The only thing that keeps me here is you. My baby girl, the only love left in my life. I've needed you, but we've never had a close relationship. For sixteen years I've been watching you, loving you from afar. Saw you grow up into a beautiful young lady...one like me, but smarter, more well-adjusted to the heavens above. I hope sometimes, maybe, just maybe, the life you've lived has made you a better, more worldly person. But then, I'll look outside and see a group of kids walking down the street, laughing, wearing more fashionable, show-off clothes, and I know the truth — it's made you less likely to understand the lives of others. I don't know any of your friends. You've had no serious relationships....I, I just haven't been able to teach you the..." and my mother broke off the most amazing sentence I'd ever heard, because of a noise in the hall. Father was home. Dinner wasn't ready. I hadn't changed. And Mom was left sitting with a look of wistfulness, regret and love on her face.

"Hello, dinner smells lovely. What time are Joseph and Reese arriving?"

He kissed my mother's forehead. But this time, I noticed how it was more out of habit and not out of love, but a simple gesture that kept my world seemingly wonderful. He sat down and glanced at the stove, then at my clothes, then around at the messy kitchen. "And what have we been doing, to keep us away from the household chores? It simply looks the way it did when I left this morning. Why are you not dressed, Anadita? And my dear..." he started, but then something caught his eye and he stared past my mother, out the window.

"Finish making our dinner. Anadita, change your clothes. Then we'll sit down to a nice dinner. After they leave, you MUST tell me why your skills have gone down to a nothingness, unnoticeable."

"After dinner," he said. I watched my plans for a normal social life fly out the window. Apparently, we would not be discussing my little party invitation. His temper was presently rising and I probably should have made my exit then and there. But I was riveted by the sudden perception I had of the tenseness between them, now that my mother and I had spoken to each other, for the first real time in my life.

Dipali K. Murti
Mentor

a moon of pluto (excerpt)

He thinks he's seventeen. When she tells him he is twenty he just looks at her with a sad confused look as if she is just being cruel. He can't remember anything that has happened in the last four years. She can't imagine how it feels to lose time. She gets freaked out enough when she's passed out and lost two minutes. Or when she sleeps late and she's lost the morning, but at least she knows she's missed that time. He doesn't know. She tries to tell him, but he doesn't remember what she says the next minute. He keeps asking her if he will get his memory back. She is getting irritated because she has already answered that question a million times, but for him it is the first time and she has to remember that.

Devika has decided to help them both. While Lars is in physical therapy, she pulls out the craypas and the drawing paper she brought for him. She writes the following words in purple. YOU WILL GET YOUR MEMORY BACK. Then she surrounds it with blues and reds and yellows and greens. When he gets back, she shows him the sign. She tells him that whenever he wonders if he will get his memory back he should look at the sign above his bed where she has placed it. But he doesn't remember that she's told him that. So he continues to ask. But at least now, she just points to the cheerful sign above his bed. Then he turns back to her and smiles his big chipped-tooth smile.

Each night they write in his memory book. Together they try to remember the events of the day and he writes them in his book. Devika does the remembering and Lars does the writing. She finds herself getting annoyed that he doesn't remember or write faster. She thinks she needs a sign. YOUR BROTHER HAS A BRAIN INJURY. GIVE HIM A BREAK.

*At the Fiction
workshop, we
experimented
with unusual
settings for our
characters.*

Veronica Sandukhtyan
Age 15

my friend lenny

I ran into a close personal friend of mine, or should I say he ran into me? Actually, he ran into my stomach. My close friend Lenny joyfully lives in the jungles of my stomach. He swims with a bright smile on his face from morning to day to night. As he swims he passes recently gobbled up cheeseburgers and titanic amounts of blue, white, minted toothpaste. He screams with delight to the scent of green broccoli with some fruity bubblegum on the side.

Lenny loves sports, especially the convenient water polo. Yup, all he needs is a net made out of strips of lettuce and a whole, luscious, red tomato performing as the ball. Lenny needs teammates, and that's where Bob and Sally come in. Although Lenny's a little greener, a little skinnier, and a little weirder, he doesn't feel bad because in my circus of a stomach there's no discrimination. Tolerance gushes out through every zesty orange, every shiny apple and yummy food I swallow.

Lenny also loves to read. He finds wonderful books in the free library floating around. Pages and pages of writings that had been gobbled up in my younger, hunger-stricken years are now manuscripts to enlightenment.

The best thing about my friend Lenny is the fact that he has a fascination with disco dancing. I mean the real stuff, the John Travolta *Saturday Night Fever* disco dancing. He has crazy boogie shoes that he made out of paint polish chippings and rubber band disasters. He jumps around doing the hustle, the boogie and the funk, which basically adds to the fact that he literally runs into me.

Lenny and I go back a long way, and even though one day I happened to try a little mini fish sandwich, he holds no grudges.

Jen Shiman
Mentor

nothing rhymes with orange

Nothing rhymes with orange!

That said,

I'm gonna write this poem

about the color red

instead.

Erin Aycock
Mentor

Stemming from a short story Corrie wrote for her English class, we decided to create imagined journal entries for some of our favorite historic characters.

william faulkner's journal

January 1936 – Oxford, Mississippi

I will drown him again, destroy him again, I will cover him, for good this time. He was resurrected because, like him, I cannot seem to let go of failure. I've studied it, internalized it, I understand but cannot accept it. Something in me still seeks salvation – for Quentin and for myself. But I cannot buy back his soul, or any of ours – the things that made them full are dusty and broken. So I will murder him once more, this time with my own hands. He will pay the reparations for all our failures and I will stand over his body and drink to my life.

Estelle is quiet – she tiptoes about the house and peeks around corners and silently empties the garbage pails I fill with bottle after bottle. I'm sure she will send me away soon. Jill is at a tender age and Estelle will not subject her to me for much longer. I would tell her that I'll be done in a few weeks, but I'm sure that putting deadlines on my own drinking binges would look to her like another sign that I need help. Three more weeks is all I need. Three more weeks to drink them all away so I can start fresh with new ghosts. For now I will sit here quietly and fill up another glass another glass another glass – and wait for her to find the strength to send me away from Rowan Oak.

WF

Corrie Siegel
Age 18

f. scott fitzgerald's journal

1923 March 3RD

I can't seem to get this book finished. The more I need to finish it, the harder it gets. Writing down the moments is the worst part. The fleeting moments that cascade down into silence like the beads of a flapper's dress in the last step of the Charleston. Like the streetlights that breathe in Zelda's hair as we are driving through Manhattan in the early morning.

I hate this. Writing a book is like a hangover, falling down from a moment in an attempt to write it. I want to capture everything. There is the paper, these memories and me. I can't think. The notes of jazz tumble through my memory as if they are falling down the staircases in my mind.

Zelda had another dream. She dreamt darkness swallowed her, and then something about a dress. Things are getting worse between us. We fight. I don't know why. I need to write a few short stories, need to get some work done, have to pay the bills.

But Gatsby is haunting me. I need to finish him. Last night I saw his future. He will die in despair. Haven't worked out the details. But, I need to know how we will end. There are always these deadlines. I am so tired. Last night I danced so much I felt as if I would collapse. For some reason I couldn't keep up with the wild step. Those movements. It was like the light in Zelda's eyes last night when we had the fight.

I can't remember what it was about, I can't remember the dance steps either. I'm forgetting them. Forgetting the moments and they are settling like ticker tape in the last hours of the night.

FSF

Amy Forstadt
Mentor

At a coffee shop
writing session,
Lena and I
selected someone
at random and
wrote from
his or her
point of view.

sunny side up

In high school, the boys called me names and shoved me into the bathroom wall. I didn't get it. I kissed popular girls. I started on the basketball team. I said swore and spit like every other guy.

How did they know before I did? Did they see me not looking at them in the showers? Could they tell what I thought about alone, at night? Did they know I was a prisoner of my own furtive glances and cold cheerleader kisses?

My mother freed me. The morning after high school graduation she marched into my room, stood on her tiptoes in my closet and handed me my battered suitcase. "Go," she said, "go somewhere and meet someone. Meet..." and here, she swallowed, "...meet a boy who's as special as you are." She kissed me on the cheek and murmured, "Don't worry. I'll tell your father."

I packed the old suitcase and drove to California. Los Angeles. The sun shone on me all the time, even when it was raining. I ate frittatas and tofu burgers. I grew a mustache. I met lots of special boys. I put on a feather boa and marched in a parade.

My mustache is gray now and my muscles are faded. I have only one special boy and he's here across from me, finishing his eggs on this sun-filled patio full of the murmur of families and the amiable clinking of silverware.

A toddler waddles by on his chubby legs, exploring the spaces between tables. I want to reach down and cradle his sweet face in my hands. I want to lean down and whisper in his tiny ear, "Be who you are."

Cheyenne Pierce
Mentor

hello lie

Hello Lie,

How are you today? And please tell the truth, ah ah! Just stop right there. I am writing you this letter to express my feelings to you and all the hurt you bring to the truth. You are so very special because you come in several forms and fashions. The white lie, the save-your-face lie, the lie without the intent to harm, and the withholding of information lie. Whatever it is, it's a lie. And I wish you would just tell the truth.

Shawna Herron
Age 14

the adventures of mantis

Here begins the story of Mantis the Dimwitted on a desert island...

Mantis Correli has been stranded on that darn island for one entire week. It all began with the Alaskan cruise ship that went down, leaving Mantis isolated away from the crew members who were too mean to let him into a life boat. Mantis had spent his time sulking and was staring out into the vast ocean and working on another sulk, when all of a sudden a bottle washed up on the shore in front of him.

"Huh?" he said, baffled at the appearance of the bottle. It held a rolled-up piece of paper and a pencil. Mantis pulled out the paper and read the note written on it.

> Dear Mantis,
> I see the predicament that you are in is tedious and right now I am guessing that you want OFF, right? It is possible, but, for a knucklehead such as yourself, it might prove almost impossible. Anyhow, I sure hope that you figure out a way to get that sorry butt of yours off this island, although I would be much surprised.
> Sincerely, Nobody

Mantis was very confused and at the same time relieved. If this guy knew his name and what he wanted, maybe he was some sort of miracle worker. Mantis shook the pencil out of the bottle and wrote on the back of the note.

> Dear Nobody,
> I get the drift. You're some sort of miracle worker, right? And what do you mean, much surprised? I'll get my butt off this island even if it's the last thing I do!
> Sincerely, Somebody

Mantis threw the bottle back into the surf and sat down to wait. Almost instantly, a huge wave crashed onto the shore in front of him, washing up what appeared to be the very same bottle as before, but with a different piece of paper in it.

Dear Mantis,
Please don't even TRY to be smart with me. I know everything,
so don't you dare try anything. I feel deep pity for you, so I'll tell
you how to get off the island. Just walk inland until you see it,
until you see…(mystic aura)…
Sincerely, The Always-Anonymous Nobody

Mantis didn't think twice. He immediately turned and started walking into the fierce jungle as the sun went down. As he walked farther and farther, he could hear the beat of music, and, as it grew darker, saw the flash of strobe lights ahead of him.

"What the…" said Mantis, confused.

"Welcome to Hilo Hawaii resort! You are Mantis, aren't you?" asked an enthusiastic waitress dressed in a traditional grass skirt and coconut bra.

"Yeah, that's me."

"Cool! You've got a letter from someone," the waitress handed Mantis a letter and went away. Mantis opened the letter.

Dear Mantis,
You should have explored the island when you first came here, Stupid.
Sincerely, God

Sheana:
We wrote this piece together. Jasmine wrote the part of the teenage girl, and I wrote the part of the mother. We discovered how much meaning can exist in subtext.

Sheana Ochoa
Mentor
&
Jasmine Benitez
Age 15

secrets & mirrors (excerpt)

Kitchen in an inner-city apartment. Mom, 32, is making a scrapbook. Lily, 16, enters.

Lily: Mom, you never talked to me about the consequences of having a kid. I think it's time you tell me about it. You never talk to me about guys and how you're supposed to act.

Mom: Guys? What do you want to know about boys? You're too young.

Lily: I want to understand what they want.

Mom: What they want. What about what you want? That was always my problem, thinking too much about pleasing the boys! How do you think I got pregnant with you at 16?

Lily: Sixteen? You met Dad when you were 17.

Mom: Who told you that? Forget it. I have this to put together. Don't you have homework?

Lily: I do have homework, but you haven't answered my question.

Mom: Look at this picture of you at the spelling bee. Do you remember that night?

Lily: Mom!

Mom: What, what question?

Lily: What do guys want?

Mom: You are too young for that!

Lily: Then just forget it, it doesn't matter now.

Mom: Yeah, you're right. You have other things to think about. Exams to pass, colleges to visit, your grades.

Lily : I won't be going to college around here.

Mom: We'll see.

Lily: You'll have to send us away.

Mom: Us? What do you mean us?

Lily: It's time for the family to grow up. Don't you think so?

Mom: What are you talking about?

Lily: Mom, I have to tell you something, but I don't know how.

Mom: Oh, no. You're not getting married. Who is this boy? Who is he?

Lily: Who said I was getting married?

Mom: Lily, I'm getting impatient with this little game. Go to your room.

Lily: Mom, I'm pregnant.

Mom: You're not pregnant. How could you be pregnant?

Lily: What makes you so sure?

Mom: You had sex?

Lily: (nods)

Mom: Ay, ay, ay. And you're pregnant?

Lily: Yeah and I think it's time for you to answer my question: what do guys want?

Mom: Why are you asking me? You seem to have that answer already.

Lily: I guess I had to find out by myself.

Mom: Did he force you?

Lily: No.

Mom: Does he want to marry you?

Lily: Don't worry about that.

Mom: So, he just wanted to get you into bed?

Lily: Thanks for answering my questions, finally.
Maybe if you had told me sooner it wouldn't be like this.

Mom: This isn't happening. You're not even 17 years old.
You're younger than I was!

Lily: What do you mean? Of course, you met dad when you were 17.

Mom: There...was another boy before him. One night...

Lily: One night what?

Mom: It only takes one night. You know that. How far along are you?

Lily: What does the boy have to do with this?

Mom: When is the baby due?

Lily: Did you get pregnant from that boy?

Mom: Have you seen a doctor?

Lily: Mom, answer my question!

Mom: Yes! Yes! I got pregnant.

Lily: What happened to the baby?

Mom: It doesn't matter anymore. It's in the past.

Lily: Is it me?

Mom: (nods)

Lily: That's why all you care about is my school. You never showed me how much you loved me. Everything has been about my education.

Mom: That isn't true.

Lily: Of course it is. Now I understand a lot of things.

Mom: You don't understand anything! What are you going to do with a baby!

Lily: I'm going to have my baby. The most wonderful thing that can happen to a woman is to have a baby, so I'll work hard to raise it. I'll love MY baby. Who is my father?

Mom: He's the man that raised you.

Lily: Who is he?

Mom: His name was Jesse. He died a few years ago.

Lily: Where is he buried?

Mom: Stop it! Stop it! Stop it!

Lily: How did he die?

Mom: This is mine. It's mine.

Lily: What?

Mom: It's the only thing I never had to share. The rest of my life has been a sacrifice, the rest of it has been paying for the little happiness I had.

Lily: Why are you telling me now! You've lied to me for 15 years. Why? Why now? Everything could have been different. Now look at me. Look at me!

Mom: I can't look at you.

Lily: No, you can't look at yourself.

Kyla Winston
Age 16

Kyla Winston
Age 16

a valid excuse

I wrote this at the Fiction workshop — we were challenged to come up with a grand excuse as to why we were late.

I was late because I broke a plate,

And a building fell, and I dropped a pail.

I was late because my dog Kernal ate my journal.

I spilled some ink and I couldn't think.

I was late because I was chased by a giraffe

and after I decided to take a mud bath.

I was late because I took a trip to the zoo...in Peru...in a canoe.

I was late because I was put back in time,

and the crazy '70s warped my mind.

I was late because I walked through a closed door

And the next thing I knew I was in a world war.

It's no debate...I was late.

I'm very sorry...

AWWW!!! I have to go now, I'm being chased by an army.

155

Kim Sudhalter:
*Kimberly and
I decided to write
a story together,
so I started the
piece using an old
newspaper article
as inspiration.
I wrote the first
paragraph and
sent it to Kimberly,
and we went back
and forth with it.
My contributions
are in italics,
and Kimberly's
are in plain text.*

Kim Sudhalter
Mentor
&
Kimberly Menaster
Age 16

fire (excerpt)

As portions of the house sank into the ground, the man appeared to shrink in his chair. The suit became two sizes too large as he clutched the tattered cardboard box in his arms.

"Sir? Sir?"

The fire captain's voice, muffled as if wrapped in a thick blanket, slowly made its way into the corner of the man's brain but he couldn't bring himself to respond.

Suddenly a shape began to form out of the smoke and ash. A statue stood, completely upright and intact, in the midst of the ruins.

"Ahhh, the Algonquin...it survives!" he shouted as he tossed Frances and her box to the ground and dashed toward the rubble.

"Sir, get away from there," the fire captain yelled. "The area's not secure!"

Mr. Emerson heard nothing but the crackle of dying flames and the rush of water whooshing through hoses as he went to claim his prize. "The statue, it's still here for me," he murmured to himself as he ran to the Algonquin's open arms.

I saw the statue and could not resist its siren call; it beckoned to me as it always had. The purity of the form, the perfection of the function, a prime example of the art that can be created. And destroyed. The Algonquin stood in its purity, its beauty. I ran over to the smoldering remains. If the statue had survived, I might.

The others in the room shook their heads, not understanding its finesse or beauty. Things that are novel startle men, yet they lead me to submission. I was the only bidder. It was left over from the estate of a poor woman, a waitress, not an artist. I do not know how she came to possess the sculpture, I was only glad that she did.

I relived the experience of finding that piece of art when I ran toward its open arms. The foolish fire captain was sending his men after me when I reached it. I knelt at the base, stroking the glorious lines with my palm. Men swarmed around me like ants and they pulled me away from its aura of brilliance.

"Sir, you'll have to go," a fireman yelled at the wizened man clutching the gaudy statue. "The gas lines are open and this thing could blow any minute!"

Mr. Emerson couldn't move. He held tight to his last remaining dream, the last vestige of his purpose. He wrapped himself around everything he stood for. His business, his life, his love were crumbling all around him but one last beacon stood clear in the burning night.

"What's wrong with this guy?" the soot-smeared fireman murmured to his partner as they approached the curious pair. One grabbed the statue and one grabbed Mr. Emerson, trying to rip the two apart. A keening wail escaped Mr. Emerson's lips as they pulled, a sound so hollow and soulless the men covered their ears to escape the pain.

"It's just a goddamn pile of junk," one yelled to the other. "What the hell's the big deal?"

Moving with a new sense of purpose, Mr. Emerson shook the men in the yellow slickers from his shoulders, and began to try to lift the Algonquin. "She must be saved," he breathed as he positioned his hands under her outstretched arms. With every ounce of strength his frail body could marshal, he struggled to raise the marble form off the ground. It would not budge. He repositioned, hoping to gain better leverage, but the statue refused to release its hold on the earth.

I pulled with every ounce of my remaining strength. The statue did not want to move. It beckoned for destruction. It breathed an end. I stood back and relaxed my grasp. I gazed at the statue and a tear dripped down my cheek. I allowed myself to be pulled back by a faceless fireman.

The statue was incinerated.

And as the hideous statue crumbled, Mr. Emerson sank to the ground, seeming to melt into a faceless, formless puddle. Where a once proud lover of all that is beautiful had once stood, now lay a sodden pile of garments. The black and white of the tuxedo blended in with the gray ash that now blanketed the ground.

Firemen scurried back and forth, barely noticing that a man lay dead in their midst. Out of the confusion, a small form emerged. Mr. Emerson's cat made its way serenely through the clouds of dust to sit on the dirty heap that was once his master.

Meghan McCarthy
Mentor

As a writing exercise, Gaby and I decided to make up bogus instructions for housesitting. We didn't realize until the end that we both chose to write about similarly ridiculous things.

housesitting letter

Dear Gaby,

Thanks so much for agreeing to housesit while I am on my six-week around-the-world in a hot-air balloon tour. I would not be able to fulfill this life-long dream if it weren't for you. And the California lottery. And my parole officer's willingness to take a bribe. But mostly you. Below you'll find a list of things that I need you to do for me while I am gone:

1) Feed the fish. Unfortunately, I have raised half-a-dozen very finicky eaters. They have acquired a taste for filet mignon and I'm afraid nothing else will do. Believe me, you do *not* want to substitute another kind of meat. Piranhas are not the kind of fish you want to see angry. I did mention my little guys were piranhas, didn't I? But don't worry. They are practically harmless. Unless you show fear. So don't. Really, I'm not kidding on this one.

2) Water the plants. This one is pretty self-explanatory. You'll just need to sneak into the next-door-neighbor's yard and hook a hose up to the spigot. My water bill has been a little out of control lately and that old lady is so crazy she will never notice a few extra gallons on her bill. Just ignore the "Beware of Dogs" sign on her fence. You're young and will have no problem outrunning a couple of Doberman pinschers. Also, don't stand too close to the flesh-eating begonias. They are a science project I have been working on in my spare time and I haven't yet determined the best way to pull them off of their victims.

3) Keep out of the attic. Don't ask why. Just don't go in there. I can't have that thing escaping again. It will just be bad for everyone.

I really appreciate your help. Please feel free to help yourself to anything in the kitchen. Except the filet mignon. You do not want to get on the *flying* piranhas' bad side. I did mention they were flying piranhas, didn't I? Anyway, I'll see you in six weeks. Thanks!

Your friend,
Meghan

Gabriela Cardenas
Age 14

housesitting letter (excerpt)

Dear Meghan,

You recently told me that you have a lot of time on your hands so I sat down and thought long and hard. Finally, it hit me. Why don't you take care of my house while I run away from the FBI? I know I can trust you because you are a very dependable person. (Cough, cough...)

I know what you're thinking. You're thinking about that time when I ran away from the CIA and asked you to take care of my house. But you don't have to worry...I don't have pet alligators anymore. Well, except sweet Fangs, but I still can't find him anywhere.

Taking care of my house won't be too hard. You just have to know where your life is in danger and where it is not. For example, you're free to hang out in my living room as long as you don't touch the floor. See? Simple.

I don't want you to get hurt so just stay out of the second floor completely. There are just too many things on that floor that can get loose and terrorize the town. Besides, I'm saving those things for special occasions. Anyway, to make a long story short, stay away from the second floor.

Last, but not least, don't forget to feed my wonderful, seven feet long Venus Fly Traps. Remember, the girl Venus Fly Traps are on the left side of the room and the boy Venus Fly Traps are on the right side of the room. The girls only eat lean meat of any sort and the guys don't care what you give them. But make sure David (the smallest one in the group) gets a bigger share than the other plants or else he'll become angry and hurt. I won't stand for it if I find out David has been crying again!

Well, I guess that's all you need to know. I don't know when I'll be back, but I'll try to send letters often. Give all my plants my love!

See you later,
Gaby

Clare Sera
Mentor

Gloria and I decided to rewrite the story of Cinderella, putting each other in the title role. We wrote the following stories sitting across from each other giggling and amped up on caffeine.

gloria-ella

The clock struck midnight and Gloriarella ran quickly from the ballroom, leaving behind one of her beautiful glass running shoes. "Quick! Quick! Go!" she cried to the footmen at her carriage. But they weren't quick enough for Gloriarella, so she sprinted home herself, beating her own best time of two miles in ten minutes, twenty seconds. And that with one glass sneaker on.

The next morning, Gloriarella got up early to study for her chemistry and fireplace-cleaning test. She aced it, and after her chores were done she laced up her ratty old (canvas) sneakers and went for her usual six-mile run.

While she was gone, the Prince stopped by her home. He was searching the kingdom for whoever might fit the glass sneaker.

Gloriarella's sisters, although slim, both had extraordinarily fat feet. But they managed somehow to each squeeze a fat foot into the shoe. That, however, wasn't enough for the Prince. "Only the girl who can run in this beautiful shoe will be my bride." Both sisters tried. Both sisters wobbled and fell.

Prince Carlos left the house disappointed. His footman directed him to the royal carriage, but Carlos wanted to walk. "Walk?" asked the footman incredulously. "Yes," replied the handsome Prince, "I need to go for a run and get the stink of those sisters' fat feet off of me."

And off he ran down the very path that Gloriarella was on, running back home. Sure enough they soon ran SMACK into one another.

"Whoa! Dude. Look where you're going," cried Gloriarella, rubbing her head. The Prince couldn't say anything, he was so taken by the sweaty beauty in front of him.

"I...uh...fffmt..." he stuttered.

"Nice to meet you, genius," laughed Gloriarella as she ran off. Prince Carlos quickly got it together and ran after her, but, by the time he reached her house, she was gone.

"She's at the Hyper Physics For Brilliant Minds lecture tonight," said her sisters helpfully, realizing the Prince was in love.

The Prince ran to the school and found the classroom. And there, in front of all the students, he got down on one knee, pulled out the glass sneaker and said, "I don't care if this shoe fits or not — you are the most dazzling woman I have ever seen. Will you marry me?"

Gloriarella looked him over. She slipped the sneaker on and pulled the matching one from her backpack. The whole class gasped. The teacher, a bit overly sentimental, fainted. Gloria smiled at the Prince and asked, demurely, "According to Van der Waal's interaction, what's the optimal distance of two identical atoms?"

"$d=2r$, where 'r' is atom radius," replied the Prince without blinking.

"Will you build my mother and sisters a castle of their own?"

"Consider it done," he said.

"Alright then. You may marry me — if you can catch me." And with that she took off running, in the beautiful glass sneakers.

Knowing he could never catch her, the Prince in the meantime built the castle for her mom and sisters and founded a university in Gloriarella's name that to this day does great research to benefit all mankind.

And there he waits, patiently, until she's ready to run home.

Gloria Espinoza
Age 17

clarella

Time's up! Her fancy gown is gone, her normal cool clothes are back, ready to do some cleaning, then writing after all the chores around the house are done. The time is one am and the stepmother and sisters are not back.

Clarella with her cool pants and matching shirt takes her time to do the dirty housework she mildly cares about because when she marries the prince she will spend her time having fun! After thinking this over, Clarella takes her soap and throws it across the kitchen.

"No! I refuse to do other people's work," she says angrily. "I am going back to the party." And with a slow and joyful dance, Clarella steps into one of her stepsisters' rooms. Looking for the perfect dress to wear, none actually fits her slim body. "Fat Sis!"

Clarella, with joy and energy, steps into her VW and leaves for the castle. While she's driving, she forgets about what she was about to do and heads straight to Florida. There she finally gets her own place to live. "And there are no rats allowed in here!" She never did like the rats that always tried to help her in the old place.

Clarella liked her new life. With no one to be her protector, she would do everything herself. She was the independent woman that many back at her old house never believed she would become.

After establishing herself and her new life in Florida, she went to Disneyworld, where she met a cool guy that was spending his day off there also. The guy worked as a carpenter for his stepfather and his brothers. Clarella told him he should come to her neighborhood and live on his own, like her.

Clarella and the carpenter spent a lot of time together. They went to Disneyworld all the time. They talked with the manager there and arranged to do some shows based on their own lives and the many characters they knew.

Clarella and the carpenter finally got married and now live happily ever after.

Gloria Espinoza
Age 17

untitled

Some day the stars are gonna eat you.

Kimberly Menaster
Age 16

*I wrote this at
2 am New
Year's Day
while watching
the movie
American
Beauty,
screaming at
Kevin Spacey
with my
best friend.*

claire

Pulsating music filled the room. The throbbing sound remained in my eardrums, a constant beat. A silver tray was balanced on my outstretched palm as I worked my way through the dance floor. Glasses were placed on it with a matter of nonimportance, half drunk with lipstick stains on the rim. Random men approached and then ran at the sight of my black and white uniform. It was more of a BEBE pinstripe vest and pants with a white shirt, but the principle remained. The tray, not the outfit, was out of place.

New Year's in a faceless bar on Sunset. I had served bar so many times at so many places that I no longer drew a distinction. There were strobe lights that compensated for the dim lighting, migraines flashed through my skull. The bar was parallel to the back wall, where several others were bartending. I was the only graduate student. I had to pay rent. I picked up one of the glasses on the tray, delicate sides holding an olive above a long stem.

I mixed a Scotch on the rocks and a margarita with the sense of routine. Orders that sound important and knowledgeable while the person has no idea what they are drinking. The liquid met a shocked mouth that tried to cover surprise

"Oww," I muttered. My stupid, painful boots. I glanced around for a superior before unzipping the sides. I kicked the boots next to the bin of ice and wiggled my toes. I can't believe I borrowed boots two sizes too small from Gina. Let that teach me.

"Miss!"

"Yes," I answered, managing a smile.

"I've been trying to get your attention."

"Now you have it. What can I do you for?"

"Scotch, neat."

I nodded and traveled to the far end of the bar, my bare feet padding the mats. I procured a glass, which I placed before him and poured Scotch.

"Anything else?"

"No," he admonished sternly.

I put my shoes back on in a split second and placed the scotch and margarita on the silver tray of disdain. I crossed the club and handed the drinks off to their owners. I circulated, taking orders and used glasses. Returning to the bar, I removed the shoes as a matter of habit and began mixing.

"Miss."

"Yeah?" It was the same guy, rotten luck.

"This service is terrible, I've been waiting again."

"Okay! That's it. I draw the line at outright criticism!"

"Refill," he said cooly, not flinching.

As I filled the order, I felt his eyes analyzing and scrutinizing my every move. I heard his silent chastisements. The drink was poured and I turned my head away. Pause.

"Sir, if it's all right to ask, what's your problem?"

"My problem. You are the barkeep with an attitude issue and a chip on her shoulder."

"Answer, but do not insult."

"My problem is nothing."

"Nothing?"

"Nothing is the problem. I can...accomplish nothing by having this conversation."

He stopped and glanced up. Mainstream clothes and mainstream haircut. A bitter glance. He left, leaving an empty glass behind. I put my shoes back on.

Jennifer Castle
Mentor

Angela and I used those free promotional postcards you pick up in restaurants as inspiration. Angela was looking at a gorgeous perfume model, and I was looking at a woman's picture taken from one of those new digital camera cell phones.

cellphone ad

Take my picture, but not on film. Take it with some new technology made of zeros and ones, something that rests on the air and can be destroyed with a careless brush of the hand. Take my picture, but keep it to yourself. I won't look at the lens, but you'll know I'm there: a smaller, sharper version of myself for you to keep in your pocket. That's okay as long as you take me to deep green places and football fields of open sky, towering trees and fortresses of stone. You'll touch fingertips with the world but hear my whisper in your ear. I guess I'm always posing, alone against a blurry background, for your camera.

Angela Song
Age 17

perfume ad

Material girl...she's very beautiful, isn't she? She has the perfect hair. Her lips are like blossoms, and her chin is very sharp. Her skin looks pure as sparkling water. Her body is a form that others would have to starve to get. And look, she has a Gucci handbag on her, too. But how about her insides? Is her heart pure as sheep's blood? Is her head filled with remarkable ideas? Does she say nice words with those blossomy lips? I don't know the answer to these questions, but now I wonder: do I still consider her beautiful?

Stephanie Bowen
Mentor

dear brave soul

Dear Brave Soul,

Thank you for taking care of Chloe and Clarke. There are just a few things you should know.

1. They like to have their food bowl filled at all times. Emphasis on FILLED and AT ALL TIMES. If their bowl is, say, half-full, Clarke (Chloe would never do this) will tear open the bag of cat food, spilling it all over the floor. After cleaning up the mess, when you're refilling the already half-filled bowl, Clarke AND Chloe will rush toward you, sticking their heads directly under the stream of kibble, causing it to spill yet again.

2. Clarke loves to be brushed, although you'd never know it by his behavior. When you take out the "love glove," his ears will perk up and tail will swing. During the first few strokes he'll swirl around in a state of bliss. But then, he will walk toward you, only to turn around and walk away, expecting you to follow him all over the apartment with that spiky, rubber glove. And he won't let you near Chloe. I usually give up after a few clumps of hair.

3. The litter box. All I can say is I'm sorry. There are two cats, one box and it stinks! Worse than the stench is the paste-like substance that covers the floor when the litter mixes with water. I recommend sweeping before doing any dishes since their box is under the kitchen sink.

Don't fret — there are rewards. Say it's a lazy Sunday afternoon — there's nothing better than lying on the couch with your nose in a book and two big, orange fur balls cuddled together on your lap. Then there's bedtime. Chloe sleeps right near your head — just close enough to let her soft purrs soothe you to sleep. Clarke stays down by your feet, keeping them warm all through the night. And if you're bored there's a bag of catnip in the cupboard. A few pinches tossed out onto the carpet will give you hours of entertainment.

Enjoy your time with my babies — I guarantee it will be one you're not soon to forget.

Mara Bochenek
Age 14

This piece came out of the Persuasive Writing workshop.

dear onion grower

I'm writing to inform you about the serious injuries caused by onions. I believe that onions are a public menace due to the chemical reaction when cutting into an onion.

When cooking with onions, you can start to cry and cut your finger off. French Onion Soup? Why couldn't it just be French Soup? Maybe if you could change the genes of the onion to not make you cry, more people would want to buy more onions.

In conclusion, there have been many injuries with the onion. And you have lost me as a customer, because last week I lost my HAND.

Thank you,

Mara Bochenek

Iris Benitez
Age 17

We visited the Skirball Museum's "It's Not OK" exhibit, which dealt with teen and family violence from the perspective of teen artists. One piece in particular — a huge, red eyeball — was very moving, and I wrote this to discover the story behind the art.

eyes of the receiver

She had enough. This would be the last time he ever laid a hand on her. She couldn't take it anymore. Every day, he comes home from work, drinks his beer and, when he's had enough, that's when it starts. Yelling at first, telling her she's useless, worthless, a whore.

She tells him to stop but the words do not slow him down. When he is tired of her cries, he hits her, trying to make her stop. But that only makes it worse. Her cries become louder, his words bitter. All she wants is for him to stop.

She's on the floor now, weak, unable to move. He is moving toward her, slowly, pondering his next attack. As soon as he reaches out to grab her, she tries to move away. But her body lays still. She doesn't realize that the yelling has stopped, his fists have ceased. Cries, loud pleas for forgiveness are over.

His body hovers over hers as she lies still. By not moving, maybe she will become invisible. Then he tries to hold her, crying, asking God to keep her safe. He picks her up and takes her to their bedroom. He lays her on their bed, like a caring parent. He covers her with a blanket, watches her sleep. He brings a damp cloth from the kitchen and wipes her bruised face.

But his efforts are not enough to make her open her swollen eyes. He hurriedly gets the phone, panicking as he dials a number.

Ten minutes later, he hears a loud knock on the door. The paramedics. They rush inside to check on the girl. They take her pulse. It seems hopeless, why even try to bring her back?

One of the paramedics steps out of the room. He asks the man to take a seat, but he already knows what he's going to hear. The man lets out a loud cry and rushes back into the bedroom, to her side. He mumbles a few words under his breath.

The paramedics tell the man that the authorities have been called. He needs to file a report. He needs to come to the hospital and explain what happened.

The man's body shivers when he reaches the hospital door. He realizes the damage he has done. A policeman stands nearby, awaiting his arrival. He is taken into a secluded room and interrogated.

He breaks down and cries. He will have to pay for the loss of the woman who loved and cared for him. His one true love.

He confesses to everything, from the cruel insults to the brutal poundings. He never felt so alone, so lost. The woman who would do anything for him is gone forever, by his hand.

*This was
inspired by the
chorus of a
popular Beach
Boys song.*

Kimberly Sudhalter
Mentor

evil angels

"What do you mean you had her born in 1964?" Angel 463 yelled. "You know she was supposed to arrive in 1955. And why am I just finding this out now?"

Angel 251 cowered, not knowing quite how to answer.

"All this time she's felt off-kilter, like she arrived late for the party...AND SHE'S BEEN RIGHT!" Angel 463's temper was distinctly un-angelic at this point, his cherubic face contorted into something never depicted on the ceiling of the Sistine Chapel.

"I'm sorry," Angel 251 stammered, "I was new then...I made mistakes."

"You bet you did, you poor excuse for a seraph," screamed 463, sweat popping out all over his sweet, round forehead. "How am I going to fix this, tell me?"

"I don't know why you're so upset, 463. What's done is done and she's none the wiser."

At that Angel 463 turned bright red, his right eye twitching violently. The silence was deafening as he tried to contain his anger. His best attempts failed.

"UPSET?" he screeched. "Why am I upset? I'll tell you why. You single-handedly screwed up the entire process, that's why. You have destroyed a system that took millenniums to perfect, that's what. If it weren't so devastating, I'd be proud that a little nothing like you managed to accomplish something so enormous."

"That's not very angelic," 251 whispered under his breath.

"WHAT DID YOU SAY?"

"I said you're not being very angel-like, 463," 251 stated more loudly.

Angel 463 turned his back on the smaller angel, crossing his arms to keep himself from committing an act his boss would not look kindly upon.

"When I turn around, I want you to be gone. And I want you to fix this thing…is that clear?"

"B-b-b-but how?"

"I don't know, and I don't care! You figure out how to get her back to her own time, or at least make it clear to her what happened. HAVE YOU GOT THAT?"

Angel 251 stared at 463's back, hoping against hope that a way out would suddenly present itself. But his mind was a big ball of yarn.

"ARE YOU STILL THERE? I CAN HEAR YOU BREATHING!" 463 shrilled.

"Goddamn it," 251 muttered as he shook his tattered wings loose. "Why can't I get this stuff right?" He gathered his robes up in one arm, and took off lopsidedly, pitching back and forth as he tried to steady himself.

"Where do we get these guys?" 463 thought as he watched the pathetic angel struggle toward his cloud.

Jahbria Pierce
Age 11

how i became the ball

The world is round

And so am I

The ball was chasing me

And it caught me

And that is how I became the ball.

175

"The best medicine in life is discovering your fears and learning from them, conquering them. Finding the cure is never easy, but you'll know when you have found it. It will be when those fears fear you."

— Ivonne Cortez, age 16

THIS IS WRITEGIRL

"In my messy life, this Saturday is what saved me."

"Once a month I get relief from my everyday life."

writegirl workshops

WriteGirl workshops are all about creative self-expression, and during the course of a season, a variety of genres are explored. The results are lively, interactive, rich encounters with writing tools, tips, techniques, exemplary excerpts and shared secret recipes. There are moments when the room is completely still except for the rustle of paper and the scratching of pens. There are other moments when the room is surging with conversation and laughter. More than anything, WriteGirl workshops represent a combined creative power and an ongoing commitment to inspire and seek inspiration.

At the end of each workshop, WriteGirls take a few moments to write some anonymous comments about the day. Here are some highlights.

Journal Writing:

capturing your stories

"Colorful and stunning examples of journals from Frida Kahlo, Sabrina Ward Harrison and Dan Eldon posted along the walls showed us how this creative personal space can be much more than words. Pictures, collage, drawing and painting can express a wide range of thoughts and feelings. Journals are a wonderful place to release frustration, a way to heal, and can be a home for revelations and insight."

"Writing in shapes or upside down, using a crayon, writing to music, capturing snatches of conversation and hiding your journal from your brother were all on our Top Twenty Things To Do With Your Journal list."

"Sometimes the world is in you."

"Today I learned that a journal does not have to read like a weather report."

"Journal writing can give you courage and also inspire others. Its contents are the gift of self."

"This workshop sparked the idea of being my own life's historian, so that when lost in a place of confusion, I have a map to guide me back to my truth."

"I learned the importance of breaking my own journaling rules, and breaking them often, in order to keep my writing and my life WIDE AWAKE."

TRY THIS:

Write a mission statement for what you want to get out of your journal. It could be a dedication to someone. It could be a list of things you want to cultivate in yourself. It could be a vision of your future.

Fiction:
finding stories everywhere

*"Today I met several new characters
who all come from different worlds,
none of them ordinary."*

*"I was introduced to so many great characters: a swallowed fish,
a hot tub bum, an archer elf, a lonely girl — they're all my new friends."*

*"I liked starting from nothing and creating
a world unfamiliar to me."*

TRY THIS:

Write about a place in the world that interests you and
describe the land, the weather, the people, and what it would
be like to live there. Use all of your senses.

Creative Nonfiction:
personal stories

"We wrote everything from our favorite recipes to a short 'how-to' list. The intense writing was so contagious, once I set my pen to my journal, I couldn't stop. I loved to hear all the creative stories — it shows you more about the personality of the writer. Even though they were personal stories, we all added a bit of humor to them, and I learned this can spark things up and attract many more readers than just a simple story."

"Each of us is brimming with creative real-life stories inside and now I have ideas about how to start telling them."

"This day allowed me to realize that there is magic in nonfiction. I had always thought magic was just for fantasy or poetry."

TRY THIS:

Write a paragraph about a family member you see often. Write about their day, their routine or simply how they are at the dinner table. Use and choose your words with style and purpose.

wanda coleman

"She's coming, she's coming!" When Wanda Coleman ducked her head into the room full of nervous female energy, all talking ceased. WriteGirls had been anxiously awaiting the arrival of "The Ebony Amazon," and most of the girls had never encountered a poetic presence quite like her. Coleman grew up in South Central, L.A., and as a young, single mother, became involved in social organizations set up in 1965's post-Watts rebellion. She renders her working-class characters, drawn from a cross-section of local communities, in gritty, yet compassionate portraits of urban life. 'Round this neighborhood, she is a highly regarded successful home girl.

When Wanda Coleman stood center stage and let her voice ring out, it didn't take long for the girls to see why she is considered one of Los Angeles' most outspoken literary treasures. Coleman shared powerful poetry, writing tips and personal anecdotes with the mesmerized workshop participants. She transformed encounters with a robber at a convenience store and headstrong rodents into unforgettable characters with unique perspectives on survival. Wanda's passion and unshakeable self-esteem set a formidable example for everyone present. The room vibrated with creative energy long after she'd left, inspiring all to delve into the afternoon's writing adventures with abandon. Afterward, during the closing experiment, many of the girls and adults expressed newfound or rekindled enthusiasm for poetry and a special appreciation for having witnessed Wanda Coleman perform her work.

Poetry:
creating moods & images

*"Today reminded me how important poetry is to my soul and gave
me the opportunity to meet one of my favorite poets."*

"Your secrets are stories that only you know how to tell."

"Poetry is the only shortcut to the soul that I know."

*"Poetry is a way to let your emotions
and senses flow and it is also a way to
let your imagination run wild."*

*"Poetry is like a sophisticated diary — more powerful, more
ambitious. It brings out the light in me."*

TRY THIS:

Write a poem about a part of your body that you love.

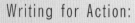

Writing for Action:

persuasive writing & letters

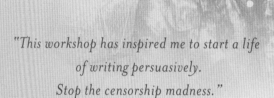

*"This workshop has inspired me to start a life
of writing persuasively.
Stop the censorship madness."*

"The girl power of the pen is even stronger now! Who could say 'no' to any one of us?"

*"I'm gonna sit right down
and write myself a letter."*

*"Even if others don't agree,
always let your views be heard."*

TRY THIS:

Write a list of things that really bug you.
Then review your list. Do you see a pattern?

Songwriting
when words are not enough

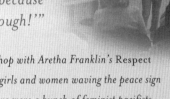

"I liked the mission for today: 'Today is about expressing how I feel, keeping it real and putting rhythm with my words, because words alone are not enough!'"

"Anyone walking into this workshop with Aretha Franklin's Respect reverberating off the walls and girls and women waving the peace sign in the air would have assumed we were a bunch of feminist pacifists inciting a new generation of Girl Power. Well, aren't we?"

"I heard a WriteGirl express her anger and realize it was OK!"

"Writing music is the only thing that makes me happy. I felt today it didn't matter if someone hates rap, pop, rock or whatever. It was just amazing that everyone had the courage to express themselves in every way imaginable."

"Verse, ramp, chorus, tag, bridge. Take these and you've got the shell of a song. Insert thoughtfully crafted lyrics, an acoustic guitar and WriteGirl talent, and you've got yourself a musical masterpiece!"

"I have all these rhythms pop-pop-popping in my head. Who knew songwriting could be so fun and easy?"

"We are not only female writers, but we are female writers who can carry a tune."

185

TRY THIS:

Write a lullaby to a small child. Think about what kind of rhymes and rhythms would be soothing.

Journalism:

perspectives on the world around us

"Today was most excellent. It's great to be with these awesome females (scheming to take over the world) and all their positive energy. At a time when everything was unraveling, it was nice to have today be the day — a new beginning — when everything comes back together. I want to be a journalist!"

"Thank you for encouraging the maintenance of a positive relationship with editors — we are not all evil! Some of us are actually helpful."

"It's tough to be objective!"

"The day flew by. So many provocative questions!"

"Wonderful to hear from people on the front-line of journalism — an inside perspective."

"Interviewing characters for a feature story was a great exercise, and it gave me a good perspective of what a journalist does. This workshop made me think about being a journalist when I grow up."

"Multifaceted and educational on all levels. I learned not only tips on how to write, but also picked up pieces of knowledge on current events, politics and gender issues."

TRY THIS:

Interview the owner of a store in your neighborhood. Prepare open-ended, provocative questions to encourage them to tell their story.

Comedic Writing:
connecting through laughter

"If funny were a smell, this room would stink! Yay WriteGirls!"

"I think from now on we should ALL wear our underpants over our clothes and start a new trend."

"Comedy is being dressed in a nightgown in public."

"Raucous laughter was at the heart of a day spent unlocking the secrets of comedy writing. Mo Collins, a fabulous comedienne from MADtv, shared her behind-the-scenes secrets of how to create comic characters and brought one of the girl's comedy sketches to life on the spot. Laughter is the best medicine and at this workshop the girls learned how to express their personal cure."

"A dog talking to a hat, a snail arresting a whale — who would have thought dialogue could bloom from such characters? What fun!"

"Wow! I knew we were all great writers, but who knew we were so funny?"

"The comedy writing was hard, but scoring a brownie after lunch was harder."

TRY THIS:

Think of two opposite characters (for example, a vegetarian and a door-to-door pork salesman) and put them in a situation where they have to talk to each other (such as a blind date). Have fun with the differences in the characters voices as they attempt to communicate.

*"It's great to be in a group that is so supportive, open and helpful.
I wish I had a WriteGirl to mentor me when I was younger."*

*"In a sometimes remote city, it's wonderful to meet other great women
and have this chance to create something unique
— beneficial to both mentor and mentee."*

mentoring

WriteGirl's mentors are all accomplished writers who are
eager to share their enthusiasm and experience with teen
girls. Pairs are matched based on mutual writing interests,
from a shared love of poetry to a fascination with the art of
screenwriting. Through weekly one-on-one writing sessions,
mentors and mentees give each other encouragement,
challenges and fresh perspectives on the craft of writing
creatively. The mentors get mentored too!

Chris Culler
Mentor

about a writegirl

I have always considered writing to be a solitary experience, something you do holed up in a room, a room of one's own if one is lucky, or in some quiet outdoor space. In that room, you wrestle with words, sentences and paragraphs; you face off with writer's block and overcome it, and you write and write and write. Thus, when I joined WriteGirl I knew I would have the Write part down. But what about the Girl part? I hadn't a clue. Having no children of my own, I had high expectations of passing the great inspirational force of writing on to future generations. But then I met Susanna, my mentee, and discovered something I didn't expect; that she would inspire me.

Susanna and I met at the WriteGirl workshop on creative nonfiction. She had come to the workshop with a group of girls from a foster home called the Chatsworth House. She had long straight brown hair, Cambodian parents, soft doe eyes, and an easy smile. Speaking in street slang (I been doin'...It don't make no...don't nobody but), she told me she wanted to get a degree in psychiatry so that she could help and counsel others. She knew about counseling, I would later learn, since she had been getting plenty of it already. She had been removed from her home by social services. "My dad and I get into fights sometimes," she later told me. At the workshops, she was an eager participant one minute, then, in the blink of an eye, tired and weary. She had worries, this girl. Big worries.

At the next workshop on persuasive writing, Susanna and I were matched-up into a mentor/mentee team. When she didn't want to participate in the workshop experiment of writing a persuasive letter to someone, I wheedled and nudged her until she finally wrote a persuasive letter to God. In it, she begged forgiveness for being "bad," and as we read it together, tears welled in her eyes. I was flabbergasted. I didn't

189

know what to do but hug her and say it was okay. This girl with the big slow smile and soft honey voice — what had made her feel so guilty and responsible? Why was she so sad? I asked her this, but she was not forthcoming. Susanna was a private person, but I hoped that the mystery of who she was and how she ended up at a foster home might be uncovered through her writing. And so, we began by working on her letter to God, and I suggested that she move the part about asking forgiveness to the beginning of the letter where she could get His (Her?) attention sooner. Get to the point. Don't ramble, I said. She laughed and agreed, and the last sentence was moved to the beginning.

A letter to God was a start, but what about Susanna's own story? "You're important," I said. "What you've been through and who you are is of interest to me and to others." She looked at me skeptically. Here I was telling this girl who felt so powerless that writing would empower her. Did I believe it? Yes! Had writing changed my life? Empowered me? Sure. I was earning a living doing it.

Over the course of the next couple of months, I met with Susanna on weekends at the Chatsworth House, a ranch-style home in a cul-de-sac in the Simi Valley area set amid horses and wildflowers. I could tell that there were strict rules at the house and that, despite the problems with her father, she wanted to go home. I cajoled her to write, even though writing wasn't at the top of her list of priorities. More than ever, I wanted to know Susanna's story, but that wasn't necessarily what I was there for. I had come to Chatsworth House to mentor her writing. But then, what was writing about anyway if not telling stories?

I saw at one of the workshops that Susanna had written "Love Is Pain" on her arm, and so I suggested that we write a poem about what it means to both of us. I asked her veiled questions on note cards: "Love Is Pain because..." "My mother is unique because..." "I hate war because..." "I miss my family because..." She wrote on the same cards, and out of her answers her story emerged: Susanna's Cambodian parents escaped the Khmer Rouge; there have been inevitable clashes between the parents and their American-born teenage daughter; Susanna spent time in Juvenile Hall. From these revelations our joint poem entitled, "Love Is Pain," emerged.

More than simply an intellectual perception, I have come to a visceral understanding that writing isn't only about words and sentences and paragraphs composed in a solitary room. It's about people and their stories. WriteGirl is about Girls. Young girls, older girls, young women, older women. I joined WriteGirl determined to teach a girl about the intricacies of writing and ended up hearing a deeply moving story about not just any girl, but a uniquely special girl. Thank you, Susanna, for telling me your story.

I want to open myself to new ideas, to dream without sleeping, to create a new dimension to which I and only I hold the key. To escape into a world with no boundaries and no limits. To reach the sky without ever leaving the ground.

Marlynne Carrera Mentee

I wanted to improve my writing and critical thinking skills. I also liked the idea of creative writing — I didn't really get that in school. WriteGirl has helped me appreciate my own work. What I enjoy most about WriteGirl is having a mentor who helps me improve my writing. Cassandra is a beautiful and talented person. I've learned — and I keep learning — from her.

Maria Santa Cruz Mentee

In order to push Maria, I have to make sure I'm pushing myself first. When I talk to her about overcoming fear and doubt, I am also talking to myself.

Cassandra Lane Mentor

I love when we're writing, just staying quiet, and hearing the sound of the pen moving and moving...I like it a lot.

Gloria Espinoza Mentee

Lovely Umayam
Mentee

my writegirl experience

I never thought that I had the ability to write short stories, songs and articles. To me, all of my poems were merely scribbles of ramblings only my mind could understand. I didn't have the confidence to believe that I could express myself because I thought no one would understand the delightful feelings or painful emotions I was trying to convey.

During my 8th-grade year, I took my writing for granted, did what was required for school and little more. I was alone without a voice, desperate for a sudden uplift from my mundane life. I needed a lot of guidance to support me and tell me that, somewhere within, there was talent waiting to be discovered and shared with others. I found that guidance when I joined WriteGirl.

At first, I had no clue what WriteGirl was about. I was reluctant to join; it was something new, and I didn't know if I would be accepted. I didn't know if I would be good enough or if I was strong enough to adjust if I did not fit in. But when I attended my first WriteGirl workshop and met my mentor, Allison, my thoughts about the program changed.

Of course, the first ten minutes were tense. I didn't know anyone and I was too shy to speak up. But then I started to loosen up, smile, laugh and write with confidence. At that moment, I realized that the other girls had the ability to express themselves through writing with the help of WriteGirl, and now, I would have the chance to gain that ability, too. It was a new sense I discovered – poems and stories became more than ramblings. They became powerful languages, condensed into special words.

Then, I started working with my mentor one-on-one. She reviewed my poems and loved them. She said that I was quite a writer. I was surprised. No one had ever told me that before. Allison helped me realize that writing was not just a hobby, something to amuse oneself, but that it was a gift and, when used wisely, it can be a powerful, creative path to self-expression.

Allison immediately became a source of inspiration and I'm glad to have a great mentor to lead me throughout my WriteGirl years. The monthly workshops are also very fun and helpful. Every time I attend, I feel the intense power and enthusiasm the women have. Everyone is eager to write and challenge herself to become a better writer. I became proud to be a part of WriteGirl and my eagerness to write and discover new things only grew stronger.

With two of my works published in *Threads*, the first WriteGirl anthology, and two more in this book, I feel very lucky to have had the chance to speak out and find my sense of self, all from joining WriteGirl and working with Allison. It has been a privilege for me from the start. If it were not for this program, I wouldn't have written my poems and stories with such confidence. I would not have shared my writing with others, especially in public, as I did at the WriteGirl readings. I would not have opened up to my own talent for literature. And after being a part of WriteGirl for almost two years, I'm still striving to write more, work harder and create.

Shawn Schepps
Mentor

mara and me

I didn't have a mentor growing up, in fact; I met my first and only mentor two years ago, John Rechy, author of *City of Night*.

I want to be a better writer, always. But, I never had a teacher who inspired me. I wasn't looking for a mentor. I imagined that mentors were for the young and impressionable, and maybe I had missed the mentor train. But as the subjective "they" say, "When the student is ready, the teacher comes." And let me tell you, that is so true.

John Rechy is a fiction writer, journalist, professor at USC, playwright and a Los Angeles icon. He's had 12 novels published, and *The Life and Adventures of Lyle Clemens*, "a modern novel inspired by Tom Jones," is due out soon. John teaches weekly workshops.

At first John intimidated me; he is quite imposing, well read, well spoken, highly intelligent and fierce about his creativity. But, after the weeks went on, I settled into the workshop and soaked up his wisdom. One night he pulled me aside and gave me a compliment, which I deflected. He looked me straight in the eyes and said, "If you don't accept your 'specialness,' it will go away, bit by bit. If you accept it, you can go from there." John wasn't only teaching me, he was seeing me. His words helped me to remember to value myself, and he officially became my mentor.

John's influence on me as an artist got me thinking. Since I was a kid who had needed someone, maybe there was a kid out there who needed me, too. When I was a teen, my parents had a bad divorce and I acted out. I cut class, got in trouble, and did things I ain't gonna write about here. I wanted to be like my mentor. I wanted to give someone the feeling of power that he gave me.

In October of 2002, I came to my first WriteGirl meeting. I was psyched. Who would my mentee would be? One by one, women and girls were being matched up in an airy room at the Bresee Center in Koreatown. I hoped my mentee would like me. I hoped that I could teach her a little something. I hoped we would find something in each other so we could learn more about life.

When they pointed Mara out to me and said, "Shawn, that's Mara, she's your new mentee," I felt kind of scared. There she was, sitting alone, waiting for me. A lanky, fourteen year-old who drew designs on her hands with a black felt tip pen, wore a Rolling Stones t-shirt, and colored her fingernails with markers. She was punk. She was rock 'n' roll, and she was funny. She reminded me of me at that age. It was a perfect match.

One afternoon Mara showed me a poem she had written on a scrap of paper called, "Teardrop." It goes like this...

The teardrop
came down on the window pane
and it rolled onto my cheek
where it fell into my hand
where I gave it to my dad
who gave it to my mom
my mom gave it to my sister
where she put it back on the window pane
and rolled off into the ground
where it went to a friend in China
and she gave it to her mom and dad
and then put it back on the window pane
and it came back to me
to keep in a jar
forever and ever
and now my jar is full of teardrops
from a friend in China.

Mara is fourteen. She clowns around a lot, but this poem shows a more thoughtful side of her. I could picture the words. I imagined a teardrop being passed from her parents to her sister to a friend in China. I could see the jar full of tears. It was powerful imagery from someone so young. A teardrop is sadness, yet she trusts her sadness with her family and even with a friend so far away. Her teardrop, or sadness, is given back to her from her friend in China, filled with other teardrops, other sadness, shared with trust. Beautiful.

Being a mentor isn't so easy. You're thrown into a situation that neither you, nor your mentee, know how to handle. You are strangers but need to become confidants, at least where the writing is concerned. I found this to be true with John Rechy, who won my trust with his own open heart and belief in me. Mentoring is trial and error.

When *Drumline* opened in theaters, I knew I would take Mara. I was the original writer on *Drumline*, with sole story and shared screenplay credit. Mara's mother had been very kind and had saved articles and reviews about the movie for me to take home after Mara and I had our sessions. I thought it would be exciting for Mara to see the movie with me and see the credits at the end. She was so pumped about it afterwards, and I felt her energy as it shot right through me. What a great way to see the film.

Mara's parents say that she's never written as much, and that makes me proud, of both of us. Pride is a gift, one that WriteGirl gives to a great many female writers. Women and girls exchange parts of themselves that may not often be heard. We support each other's efforts, and we learn how to become friends and teachers, where we were once strangers. My circle seems to have completed itself. First I found John, then I found Mara, and Mara has found me. Three generations trickling down to each other...like a teardrop that has come back from China.

the colors of painful reality

No one knew what to expect. WriteGirl's trip to the Skirball Cultural Center to view "It's Not OK," an exhibition of artwork by Los Angeles high school students addressing teen violence, was sobering and informative. Sponsored by Haven House, the first battered women's shelter in the United States, "It's Not OK" featured nearly 30 works of art, including both paper and ceramic works.

Before the group viewed the exhibit, a representative from Haven House gathered everyone into the library, where WriteGirls broke into groups and were asked to write down what the various forms of abuse could look like. One mentee said, "I found the 'physical, sexual & emotional' abuse questions and answers to be inspiring. It helped me to see how to get my way through any violent situation I might have in the future."

After some honest and intense discussion, WriteGirls went to view the work. Apparent from first glance was how each piece seemed to capture a moment in time. Pencil drawings, oils, letters and sculptures all reflected one unifying message: teen dating violence does exist and it is not okay. If any WriteGirl thought the trip involved no writing, she was mistaken! Everyone was encouraged to find one or two pieces that really spoke to them and create a story as it related to that image. Just as the artwork was filled with raw emotion, so, too were the forthcoming stories, poems and opinion pieces.

Reflecting on the field trip, one girl wrote, "It was a great combination of observation of art, discussion and writing. It also gave good advice about the way to live as a woman and a teenager in America. Expression gives us power to no longer be passive. Domestic abuse is a serious subject that faces teenage girls today and it was confronted in a very sensitive way."

jumping off the page

WriteGirls shared their passion for words with the public at Skylight Books in Los Feliz. Naomi Buckley who participated as a mentor and staff member the previous year came to support the girls and was truly blown away by how much the girls had matured. "They were so much more comfortable with their own words. They had a presence and a calm that really impressed me. What really came through was how their writing has really developed. It's strong and empowered, and I could really see how they believed in their work." Exploring creative expression is a journey that encompasses discovery, invention, revelation, inspiration and more. And as each of these girls read, they found an audience willing to listen.

writegirl,
the documentary

Several WriteGirls are creating a documentary about WriteGirl with Bresee Community Center filmmaker and teacher Jerold Kress. You can't miss them at the workshops — Pamela, Alma and Kimberly are the girls lurking behind the camera, sometimes in the shadows, other times popping up and in-your-face and always capturing all the action! Their goal is to document "the good, bad and ugly," for, as Pamela points out, "Jerold encourages us to find the drama, get the rough stuff." The girls stress the importance of documenting the truth as opposed to the promotional; their focus being to record and capture the many mentor/mentee relationships and to convey the story threads of those relationships. "Most are positive relationships," Kimberly says, "because they're here to write, and most are happy, positive people."

Aside from acquiring professional documentary techniques, the girls are also learning about the editing process. Under Jerold's instruction and supervision, they are using Final Cut Pro in Bresee's "Cyberhood," a fully equipped lab with Macintosh computers and digital video editing capabilities. "Editing is a lot like writing," Kimberly says. "You're composing one beautiful thing you're trying to convey to your audience."

Both Kimberly and Pamela are interested in future careers in filmmaking. Kimberly plans to produce documentaries on the history of Mexican and Native American peoples, while Pamela is shifting her career goals to editing and writing. Keep those cameras rolling, WriteGirls!

So Many Pens,
So Little Time

Lenise Andrade is an intern at Poets & Writers California Programs. She is using her skills as a former teacher, bookseller and bartender to raise funds for L.A. nonprofits.

Jennifer Andreone is a music marketing professional with seven years experience developing the careers of rock music artists. She is currently the Director of Marketing for Foodchain Records.

Kate Axelrod is a television writer for series including MGM/Showtime's upcoming *Dead Like Me* and HBO's *The Mind of the Married Man*. Additionally, her work has appeared in the *Los Angeles Times*, *Washington Post*, *Houston Chronicle*, *Glamour* and *Jewish Journal*.

Erin Aycock is currently a freelance Story Editor for TV shows such as ABC's *The Bachelor*. She has a BA in Creative Writing from Bard College.

Anastasia Basil is an actress and writer from Chicago. She's been nominated for numerous theater awards including the L.A. Ovation Award and has been published in *The Sun Magazine*.

Stephanie Bowen is a journalist and author. She received her Master's degree in Professional Writing from USC concentrating on creative nonfiction. She is writing a book on mentoring at-risk youth.

Jennifer Castle is an award-winning writer/producer of interactive media for young people, including *It's My Life* on PBSKids.org, and writes fiction in her spare time.

Christine Culler is a fiction writer and a story analyst at 20th Century Fox Studios.

Leslie Davis is managing editor of *Metro*, a trade magazine for the public transportation industry. She began working on *Metro* after graduating from Emerson College.

Allison Deegan is a marketing and business consultant who writes screenplays, novels and, through her involvement in WriteGirl, has recently rediscovered a love of poetry.

Heather Duffy-Stone is a writer of short stories, novel beginnings, articles, interviews and essays. Her most recent project was an anthology of poems by high school students from Los Angeles, which she edited.

Jessica Emerson-Fleming's award-winning articles have been published in various magazines; her stage play, *The Greys*, was produced last year in Hollywood, and she writes novels, poetry and, yes, screenplays in her spare time.

Sarah Fain is a television writer, currently on the WB show *Angel*. She is a former high school English and Creative Writing teacher and is an alumna of Teach for America.

For thirteen years, **Maria Elena Fernandez** has worked as a newspaper journalist in four major markets. Her children's book, *The Secret of Fern Island*, was published in 1996.

Susanne Ferrull has worked as a journalist, editor, publicist and freelance writer for more than 10 years. She holds a Master's degree in magazine journalism from Syracuse University.

Amy Forstadt writes online greeting cards for a living. She has also written several screenplays and is currently working with Jennifer Shiman (another mentor) to develop and sell an animated television show.

Mona Gable is a writer whose articles and essays have appeared in numerous publications, including the *Los Angeles Times Magazine*, *Health* and *Salon*. She also contributed to the best-selling anthology *Mothers Who Think: Tales of Real-Life Parenthood*.

Linda Gase is a television writer/producer. She has written for *ER* and *The District* and is currently working on *Wildcard*, a new drama for Lifetime.

Yvonne DeLarosa Green is an L.A. native, with a BA in Film & TV and a Master's in Screenwriting from UCLA. Yvonne is an award-winning screenwriter, currently in pre-production on one of her screenplays.

Heather Hach is a screenwriter. She wrote the upcoming *Freaky Friday* and worked at the *New York Times'* Denver Bureau and as a magazine editor in Colorado before writing for film.

Singer-songwriter **Cara Jones'** compositions have been recorded by million-selling artists, used in Playstation games and commercials and featured on her own three critically acclaimed albums.

Laurie Kaye is a television marketing writer/producer, former newscaster and music journalist. Highlights of her print and broadcast career include John Lennon's last interview.

k-lee is a Los Angeles native singer/songwriter. She is a former English, history and music teacher who volunteers with numerous organizations throughout L.A. Currently, she manages a teenage R/B singer and has a private vocal instruction business for singers.

Kari Hayes Khalil writes dry technical manuals by day and juicy fiction and poetry by night. She's currently completing a novel and a book of poems.

Kesa Kivel is a poet, teacher and activist. She has taught poetry to foster teens and incarcerated youth and now enjoys teaching journal writing.

Cassandra Lane, formerly a newspaper journalist, is working on her first book, part of which will be published by Random House in January 2004.

Cecilia Hae-Jin Lee has been an artist and writer ever since she can remember. She is currently working on a photo series and a Korean cookbook.

Singer/songwriter **Michelle Lewis** has written for and with such diverse artists as Cher, Amy Grant, Kelly Osbourne, Michelle Branch and Shawn Colvin, in addition to releasing her own solo albums.

Traci Lind is a screenwriter and political activist who has sold numerous "Go-Girl" comedies. She is also the Executive VP of Marketing & Business Development for two successful entertainment-centric Internet companies.

Princess Lucaj is a poet, filmmaker and cultural/environmental activist. She was born in Israel, raised in Alaska and currently resides in Los Angeles. She is a 1999 Sundance Fellow and a 2002 Emerging Voices/Rosenthal Fellow through PEN Center USA.

Christina Lynch is a television and film writer who is glad that debtor's prison is a thing of the Dickensian past, otherwise who would dare to be a professional writer?

Angela Mankiewicz has had two poetry chapbooks published: *Cancer Poems* and *Wired*. Recent publications/acceptances: *Montserrat*, *The Temple*, *Slipstream*, *Lynx Eye*, *Chiron*, *Hawaii Review*, *Pemmicani* and *On the Page*.

Meghan McCarthy is a former Disney Screenwriting Fellowship recipient who has scripted a comedy for Universal and a family comedy for First Look Media.

Dipali Murti is working on an MFA in Creative Writing at CalArts. Her thesis is a novel about the mythology of accidents.

Deborah Obregon is a Job Developer at the Bresee Foundation, working with teens to help them find career direction and employment. In her spare time, she is an avid journaler.

With her Master's in Professional Writing, **Sheana Ochoa** publishes in every genre from poetry to book reviews. She is currently working on a biography of Stella Adler.

Pat Payne is a multimedia installation/performance artist, poet, visual artist, reluctant shaman and self-avowed troublemaker. She holds the 2002 Taos Poetry Circus Heavyweight Title.

A failed film development executive, **Jody Paul** wrote on staff of *The Drew Carey Show* for two years. Currently she's working on a screenplay and collection of single-girl short stories.

A SoCal native born to Mexican immigrant parents, **Liliana Perez** graduated from UC Santa Cruz with a BA in Theater Arts and earned her MA in Screenwriting from AFI.

Kim Purcell has worked as a television and radio reporter in Canada before deciding to focus on fiction. She has just finished writing a thriller.

Deborah Reber is a former children's television executive who has recently shifted her career to writing nonfiction and fiction for teens and 'tweens full time.

Jennifer Repo is a former editor at Penguin Putnam Inc. One of her books recently hit the *Washington Post* best-seller list. She is currently working on a true story about a woman who has recovered from anorexia nervosa.

Ariel Robello is a poet based in Echo Park. A 2002 Emerging Voices Fellow with Pen Center USA, she is the author of *Con Ojos Claros* and founder of Full Moon Phases, a women's poetry cipher.

A native of Los Angeles, **Elizabeth Rodgers** is a screenwriter, documentary filmmaker, performance artist and gourmand, all rolled up into one.

Diana Rosen has written thirteen books, including *Meditations With Tea* (2004), writes poetry, magazine and online articles and teaches freewrite, poetry and book proposal writing.

Erika Higgins Ross is currently writing for television. Her fiction has appeared in *Stagebill*, *Juice* and *Angeleno Stories* magazines. She just finished her first novel.

With a BA from Stanford and an MFA from UCLA, **Diane Saltzberg** has written (and sold) screenplays, film criticism, campaign brochures and annual reports. She's also a freelance editor and prooofer (yes, she saw that typo!).

Shawn Schepps grew up in Los Angeles. She has written the films *Encino Man*, *Son-in-Law* and *Drumline*. Shawn just completed her first novel.

Marcia Schmitz has a Master's in Library and Information Science from UCLA. She is the Librarian/Nonprofit Resource Specialist at the Center for Nonprofit Management.

A short-fiction writer and former English teacher, **Michelle Semrad** works as a project coordinator for the Riordan Foundation managing technology-assisted early-literacy grants.

Clare Sera is a screenwriter and script consultant who has worked on projects for Dreamworks Feature Animation, 20th Century Fox and Deep River Productions. Clare has also had five plays produced and has written and performed on several comedy sketch shows for NBC and ABC.

Devorah Servi brings experience writing grants, lyrics and public relations pieces, as well as a passion for mentoring. She is the Jewish Reconstructionist Movement's West Coast Director.

Jennifer Shiman works as a Flash animator for Internet entertainment company eUniverse. She also conducts workshops on cartooning and comics. She and writing partner Amy Forstadt aim to sell and produce an original animated show.

Diane Siegel is a museum educator and writer. Previously a classroom teacher, she has a BA in English and an MS in Special Education from Syracuse University.

Julie Simonson primarily writes creative nonfiction — short stories & essays. She also coordinates an adult volunteer literacy program through the Los Angeles Public Library.

Kim Sudhalter is a communications and public relations expert who specializes in corporate branding and creating consumer products campaigns for major media and entertainment companies.

Keren Taylor, WriteGirl's Founder and Executive Director, is a singer/songwriter, poet and visual artist. She has performed her original music from Vegas to Vancouver, and she has designed and presented more than 100 creative writing workshops for youth and adults.

Rita Valencia is a writer of prose and plays whose work has been produced bicoastally and published in numerous literary journals.

Patty Waggoner is a high school English teacher with a heart of a creative writer. She writes horror fiction, poetry and creative nonfiction/autobiography.

Alisa Williams was a substitute teacher for three years. Working as a corporate trainer, she completed the book *How Can I See the Sun When It's Always Raining?*

Kim Woltmann graduated from Northwestern University in 2002 with a BA in English, majoring in Writing and Art Theory & Practice. She works at the Riordan Foundation.

writegirl leadership

Executive Director and Founder

Keren Taylor *Songwriter, Poet, Visual Artist*

Volunteer Staff — The "Engine" of WriteGirl

Sara Apelkvist
Kate Axelrod
Stephanie Bowen
Allison Deegan
Heather Duffy-Stone
Jessica Emerson-Fleming
k-lee
Nanci Katz
Traci Lind
Sarah McHale
Lori Obregon
Pat Payne
Deborah Reber
Elizabeth Rodgers
Shawn Schepps
Clare Sera
Diane Siegel

Volunteers

Renee M. Carter
Leslie Davis
Aungela Dean
Susanne Ferrull
Elizabeth Gill
Maria Gonzalez
Cara Jones
Lolo Kartikasari
Laurie Kaye
Malie
Angela Mankiewicz
Christine McBride
Dipali Murti
Wendy Nolte
Laura Rittenberg
Alisa Rivera
Dana J. Robinson
Maria Elena Rodriguez
Diana Rosen
Rani Sahota-Hans

Advisory Board

Barbara Abercrombie *Novelist, UCLA Writing Instructor, Lecturer*
Kate Axelrod *Television Writer*
Shelley Berger *Poet and Beyond Baroque Poetry Teacher*
Suzie Coelho *Lifestyle Expert, Author and HGTV Television Host*
Kai EL´Zabar *Writer, Editor, Multimedia Consultant*
Carla Fantozzi *Executive Director, ArtsCorpLA*
Elizabeth Forsythe Hailey *Novelist*
Marc Hernandez *Literary Manager, Crescendo Entertainment Group*
Sheryl Kaplan *Grants Consultant*
Vickie Nam *Writer, Editor of* Yell-Oh Girls *(Asian-American teen anthology)*
Lori Obregon *Director of Literacy & Enrichment, Bresee Foundation*
Joy Picus *Former L.A. Councilwoman, Community Organizer*
Cecilia Rasmussen *Writer and Columnist for the Los Angeles Times*
Deborah Reber *Author (Publications Chair)*
Elizabeth Rodgers *Screenwriter (June Gala Event Chair)*
Aleida Rodríguez *Poet, Editor, Educator, Translator, Publisher*
Diane Siegel *Museum Educator, Community Organizer, Teacher, Los Angeles Public Library Consultant*

writegirl supporters

WriteGirl would like to thank the following supporters, whose generous contributions made this book possible:

Bresee Foundation

Eli and Edythe L. Broad Foundation

**City of Los Angeles Cultural Affairs Departments
– Youth Arts Division**

**Los Angeles Unified School District
– Beyond the Bell Branch**

Los Angeles Times

RR Donnelley

Writers Guild of America, west

Individual Donors

WriteGirl Mentors and Volunteers

209

community connections

WriteGirl would like to thank the following for their participation and support:

Participating Schools:

Agoura High School

Belmont High School

Berendo Middle School

Beverly Hills High School

Crescent Heights High School

Cleveland High School

Dorsey High School

Downtown Business Magnet High School

El Camino Real High School

Fairfax High School

Hamilton High School

John Marshall High School

Los Angeles High School

Roosevelt High School

Thomas Starr King Middle School

Virgil Middle School

Referring Organizations:

Bresee Community Center

Children Are Our Future

Heart of Los Angeles Youth (HOLA)

Los Angeles Mentoring Coalition

Para Los Niños

Poets & Writers Magazine

Tyra Banks' TZone Camp

UCLA Extension Writer's Program

Writers Guild of America, west

Writers Guild Foundation

index of contributors

211

index of contributors

about writegirl

WriteGirl, a project of Community Partners, was founded in December 2001 in Los Angeles, bringing together talented women writers with inner-city high school girls for one-on-one mentoring on creative writing. Armed with an all-volunteer staff, WriteGirl has trained more than 100 mentors from a wide variety of neighborhoods and cultural groups throughout Los Angeles and has enrolled a diverse group of more than 100 girls, grades 8-12, representing sixteen public schools in Central Los Angeles.

In addition to establishing mentoring relationships, WriteGirl holds monthly full-day interactive writing workshops designed to introduce girls to a wide variety of writing genres, including poetry, songwriting, fiction, creative nonfiction, journalism and screenwriting, as well as public readings. WriteGirl runs September through June, culminating each year in a publication and season-end celebration for family, friends and the community. Visit WriteGirl on the Internet at **www.writegirl.org**.

Bold Ink is WriteGirl's second anthology. Its first, *Threads*, was published in 2002.